Old/New World

Peter Skrzynecki was born in 1945 in Germany and came to Australia in 1949. He has published fifteen books of poetry and prose and won several literary prizes, including the Grace Leven Poetry Prize and the Henry Lawson Short Story Award. In 1989 he was awarded the Order of Cultural Merit by the Polish government, and in 2002 he received the Medal of the Order of Australia (OAM) for his contribution to multicultural literature. His memoir, *The Sparrow Garden*, was shortlisted for the National Biography Award. He is an adjunct associate professor in the School of Humanities and Languages at the University of Western Sydney.

Other books by Peter Skrzynecki

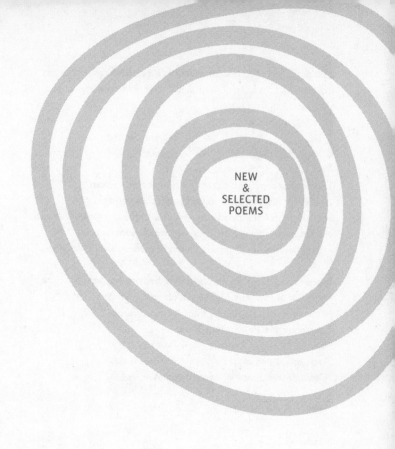

NEW
&
SELECTED
POEMS

Peter Skrzynecki
Old/New World

UQP

First published 2007 by University of Queensland Press
PO Box 6042, St Lucia, Queensland 4067 Australia

www.uqp.uq.edu.au

Typeset in 10.5/12pt Adobe Garamond by Post-Pre Press, Brisbane
Printed in Australia by McPherson's Printing Group

Cataloguing in Publication Data
National Library of Australia
Skrzynecki, Peter, 1945- .
  Old/new world: new & selected poems

  ISBN 978 07022 3586 3

I. Title.

A821.3

For Kate, Judy, Andrew & Anna

'Mojej wspaniałej rodzinie'

Acknowledgments

Thanks to the editors of the publications in which some of
the new poems first appeared: *Agenda, Australian Book Review,
Australian Literary Review, The Best Australian Poems* 2004 (Black
Inc, 2004), *The Best Australian Poems* 2005 (Black Inc, 2005), *The
Best Australian Poetry* 2003 (UQP, 2003), *Blast, Five Bells, Heat, No
River is Safe* (Poets Union, 2001), *Quadrant, Salt: An International
Journal of Poetry and Poetics, Sidewalk, Southerly, Sun and Sleet*
(Poets Union, 2006), *The Sydney Morning Herald, The Weekend
Australian, Thylazine, Ulitarra,* and *World Literature Today* (USA).

Special thanks to my family and friends for their support over the
years and to Madonna Duffy and Bronwyn Lea at University of
Queensland Press for their encouragement and editorial advice;
also to Barbara Mobbs, my literary agent, whose common sense
and laughter make the impossible possible.

Contents

NEW POEMS *Blood Plums* 2006

There, Behind the Lids

Feel the trembling, there, behind the lids,
when you close your eyes and press
index finger and thumb against the hard sockets:
against the darkness; and say whether
icebergs or black granite crags, jutting,
press back and force open your eyes

on to the glaring sun and screeching gulls
which are part of every coast we have ever visited.
And then, how it is that you will return again
to that void, regardless, assured of your safety:
what draws you upon that abyss – or perhaps
you once heard a lone cry in mid-ocean at night,

and you left? What nags and persists so greatly
that makes you the unspoken alert hero
who withdraws to the company of a small transistor,
and then learns meaning from a distant voice?
All our explanations no longer suffice, even as legend,
yet you become grander in wisdom and simplicity.

Say whether the thuddings you hear and commune with
are those the unborn child might feel while
its mother pushes a trolley through a supermarket, or
those made when damp earth is dropped on to a coffin.
Tell how we might cross over the chasms and oceans
behind our eyes: cross over, and return to new landmarks.

Listen, the Fish as They Move

for Kevin Coates

Listen, the fish as they move
from rock to weeds, and from
weeds back to rock – passing
through drifts of coldness –
they do not wince and recoil
when the crow descends upon circles
they start as they break

the surface and yawn at the sun.
Listen, listen beyond the call
of flying fox that has clung
to your mind since nightfall and prayer:
back to the music of ocean
and the honeyeaters in the brushes.
Cries, singular and many,

surround these fish – but they only
stare, dumb and spawning, return
through the dark current of rivers
to shallow clear beginnings.
Ignorant of the flooded gorges in our minds
they return – ignorant of blasphemy,
as each one yawns to swallow the sun.

By Graveyard Creek

It was almost uncanny – as if by accident
we came across that mud-brown clearing.
Alongside the bridge where fairy martins
were perched on broken, cob-webbed nests.
But we had come down on purpose: to look
for rock specimens, here, by Graveyard Creek.

The autumn sunlight hurt our eyes
as we inched along the grassy pebbled bank,
coming through olive-green walls
of sacred bamboo and frail tobacco bushes.
Further back an eagle climbed against
the wind, soared above the Lion's Head,

almost level with the top of Mount Warning.
Crows settled back into the trees
and the sound of leaves was now
matched only by children's laughter and song.
Then, below a fallen log, I saw
the green, red-spotted patches covered from the sun –

here, by Graveyard Creek: this Aboriginal place
of burial, lying hidden from the road.
We had stopped, for a minute or so, first
looking up at the eagle, now over our heads,
then across to the wild strawberries,
growing quilt-like, at the foot of the last hill.

Wallace Stevens

1

Among old text books and holy pictures
the skull has been kept for ten years now,
wrapped in white silk, hidden away.

The lagoon was knee-deep in faint light
around the edges where we were prawning.
Ten years ago, washed up on the inlet –

well-hidden under rocks and waterlily;
recovered next morning and carried
back in secret, never to be shared.

2

Taken out, year after year, held up
to a lamp and revolved: revolved
while light washed the dome, flawless, cleaner.

In ten years only the beak has changed:
fallen to one side, membrane unevenly
parted as if in annoyance or fear: splayed.

3

No winds, sand or speared fish become part
emblems of that night, of nets and sea weed,
of that gull – caught, washed from what coast?

Not even the angels of ten years ago
to whom the psalms were offered nightly:
only shells, with their trapped music,
soft, stiletto.

No Less Dark

for my mother

1

For nearly six weeks, every third or fourth day,
she would bring in flowers for my bedside
and say how they'd been specially picked
young for their freshness to last:
arrange them herself with all the care
of a celebrant laying out vestments –
red roses, sometimes entwined with jasmine,
no less dark than the blood suspended above me.

At night I would imagine the petals unfolding
in the flower room – remembering the constant drip and drip
into my arm, thinking and thinking: who was the donor?

2

Every year the garden blooms like a wild-fire,
but from now on she must tend to seedlings
that are no more hers than mine.

The Farmer

The place of birth that his relatives gave
was a little town somewhere west of the mountains;
but he hardly seemed to care whether or not
they were talking: just gripped the sides
of the cot they'd strapped him into,
and his small blue eyes followed
the orange dot on the cardiograph monitor.
When they left, tip-toes and apologetic,
he asked for water and perhaps for the leads
to be taken off: it was all too uncomfortable
like that.

Slumping back he'd watch the dot rise and fall
crazily – disappear and reappear, sometimes non-stop.
All the while his fingers strained inwards
at himself and at the black thin leads.
About twelve hours later he was dead.

He'd talked about his farm and the winds
that came off the slopes in winter:
the frosts, grass parrots, and the orchards he'd planted:
about his late wife and her love of books:
about the early years spent in northern Queensland,
till he returned and settled down after the war.

Even now his strong voice comes back
like a soft rainstorm moving in the brain –
more incisive than the high frequency pitch
of that machine when he died:
when eighty-four summers were written off as dead,
and the full stop was a fading scribbly line.

Weeping Rock

Only after reaching the bottom did we stop
and listen to the drifting echoes –
as long-dreaded farewells when words are lost to worlds
in the embrace of death: of flesh with unimagined earth.
From cracks and blotched furrows the water
trickled silver on to ferns, grass and flowers
where, bordered by moss in crevices,
icicles remained unchanged from winter frosts.

A cool spring it had been: and the same now,
miles and years and gorges away.
The rock's water seeped noiselessly into
the chasm from boulders and forests of gum –
streamed, as if the years in grief had come to claim
our presence: turn bone to rock and flesh to moss.

Wollomombi Falls

More than a thousand feet of rock face
rise slanting through a cloud of mist
and outcrops of undergrowth shadows –
photographed in all seasons, at sunset and in flood,
dusty on a rack of slides in the local
general store. Farmers graze sheep and cattle
on the brink of the chasm, and visitors
leave surrounding paddock gates open.

Chipped for specimens and dating, measured
in line with the coast a hundred miles away,
this New England monument, formed deep
into granite and ironbarks – milestone now
for winds and rain: souvenir of time and origin,
sold and bought for twenty cents.

Jeogla

Rabbits scatter in fright behind tussocks
or into the hill of a blackberry hedge
as your wheels drum over the grid of a cattle ramp.
Lowries in flocks or pairs of rosellas
quickly settle back into the cluster of ironbarks.
Grass strikes you as never being too green,
except the clover, perhaps, with a scent
which somehow gets through the dust
and haze of sunlight that vision can't penetrate –
as if a shield was reflecting the stare
of an obstinate, silent god.

Autumn and winter were mornings of grey frost
on the stubble of granite – Herefords
grazing along the roadside and barbed wire fences:
sentinels on the edge of timber ravines
or boundaries of creeks and ridges of eyesight.

Evening was a trail of smoke rising
in columns above the small tableland homestead;
stars hanging overhead, as if blossoming
from invisible branches, always just out of reach;
and always you thought of Tantalus
or the great Scandinavian ash:
found adequate words for conversation
but none for the solitude of silence that spread
over your mind as night unfolded its blanket
and you reached out for a taste of native manna.

Perhaps the roads going east someday
will bring all the answers, join coast to mountains
and people to people – make it all more than just
names on a road mailbox or the discovery
of a village that isn't on some maps:

all the backblocks where wooden floors
have witnessed lessons, childbirth and death;
where you find evidence of the seasons on the bark
of any tree – or in the eyes of a farmer
as he carries a backlog over to the hearth.

Wallamumbi

for Judith Wright

Seasons of inheritance and shadows of voices
haunt its hills like a recurring dream.
From the eastern sea a wind vanishes in snowflake,
lyre's note and the green geometry of a man's eyes –
but how does a man choose the name
that will accompany him faithfully to the grave:
become a witness to years of loss and joy,
then survive him throughout eternity?

In the ancient forest of gorges
he listened to the whisper of birds,
heard the chant of midnight prophecies
and a name spelt out into the darkness of gullies;
saw the migration of men and wings
along the frozen river in the Kingdom of the Dead:
the begin-all, end-all landscape
from which no one before him had returned,
where all mists rise, frost hardens bone,
and each granite boulder, like a stationary planet,
becomes a landmark under a galaxy of tableland stars.
Inanimate or living, he knew the migration
must continue beyond the hills he had built upon
and the slopes of his own years.

Acres of stubble became the tracks over which
his mind and heart wandered – outposts of journeys
he made, settled before sons and daughters
grew to know the poison of nettles and bull ants.
Acres he ploughed became chapters in a book
he never wrote.

Grandfather and father, remembered
from an old time, old country where it rained all summer
and native bees carried the smudge of fires

from the black honey of stumps and hollows.
Grandfather and father – man I never knew –
the name falls softly across the ranges
and paddocks that once were part of your flesh:
falls like my shadow did before the sun
on the spring morning of your death.
The chapters are still not finished
but a page is written in the Book of Change.

Styx River

If time and frost have spared these hills
why should hands curb the stream?
Deeper than sound in a bone's hollow
has the river cut into this flesh of earth.
The waterfall, crashing out of forgotten centuries,
throws up an arc from inside the sun.

In pools of thorn, deep as an eye's lens,
rainbow trout and waterhen glide
through ripples of leaves that, once seen,
wash into the mind's sleep, reshaping a dream,
unearthing the destinies of voices and stars.
Families live scattered along banks
of yellow clay, biding sleet and winds of summer
with words the colour of sunflower seeds.

I will never walk along the bottom
to disprove its name and origins – confirming
myths of Hades or the stories
brought back by men from the city.
Let myths and tales remain
in the colour and shape of trees,
in the sound of hail breaking against granite –
sunlight piercing the eyes of trout,
winds threading their needles
around tableland chimneys and doors.

Let myths remain, with their gullies and secret ferns,
and begin journeys along rivers as this
only when conscience and self
look to lands beyond the earth of hard flesh:
beyond the bridge spanning day and night
where Charon himself is a passenger
and the mouths of the dead are empty.

And you, all journeys ended, knowing time has come
for waterfalls to be silent, fall
on your knees to drink from the river.
As time and frost slowly enter your blood
no draught of hemlock could have tasted sweeter.

Moonbi Hills

Over the northern rise
you feel an air of dampness
settling onto your shoulders like a cape –
and nineteen hundred feet of skyway
point to a horizon of grey, dotted hills.
Sloping paddocks and a brown river
become reminders of a warmer season,
a different country perhaps.

Southwards, the plains – mauve edges
of a torn hat covered in dust and pebbles,
blades of grass, peppercorns and wheat –
unroll at the foot of corrugated spurs.
Coming from the top you move
to the left as the sun gathers
momentum behind you: make way
for an avalanche of trees and rocks
that falls and falls, but never leaves the sky.

Two hills: a bridge of rock,
bitumen and guideposts between climates
and winds you can pass through in the same breath –
volcanic deposits of snow and lava:
hideout for centuries of people and years,
unknown like fallen stars.

When the last diamond of snow
is mined, polished, cut and sold,
who will remember the hand that stole
fire from out of the sun:
formed two hills like rings on a broken knuckle –
and when rivers stained the tips of leaves
settled just a little further into the earth?

Small School at Kunghur

It was the children each morning
who told me of the weather,
bushfires and flooded creeks –
how not to listen to the wind or trees
when storms broke on to the roof.

In a yard lined with lantana,
camphor laurels and black wattle,
we ran races to warm up
before school started in winter –
with our voices, shot down crows and magpies
that fought in the jacarandas;
drew pictures on sheets of frost
that night had left for us.

It was the country
where the sun was always too hot.
Each morning I waited
for the mail bus and news from home,
counting banana plantations
and mountains of bougainvillaea
to pass away my time:
where blood-birds,
tree snakes and catfish
taught me a language
I was born without –
made me a stranger to my own parents
and gave me dreams that follow
like an inborn pain.

The hour before school began
I talked with farmers
as though it were a death-bed request
on my own part –

     in the country
where parents and children
spoke in a language I'd only heard about,
and the sun drained my breath
in the shade before noon:

where I sometimes started out
on the long walk home,
my slow feet over stick and leaves
with a sound of breaking ice –
wondering if life's big lessons weren't over
before the day had even begun.

Lorikeets
for Noel & Norma Howard

North from the rainforests
they invaded our trees
in their screeching flocks –

each morning, bringing summer
on green-and-golden wings, crimson breasts,
purple rainbows of outspread tails:

these nomads that lay waste
to orchards and crops – camphor laurels,
silky oaks, black bean-trees

arching with blossoms and honey.
Leaving the ground darkened
with torn leaves, branches, empty buds,

by midday they were gone
like a storm cloud – south or north
we could never tell,

as they wheeled in circles
above the valley forests
or skimmed the river like driven snow:

back and forth over a green mirror
that would not show the colour
of their eyes – leaving a forecast

of hail or mountain fires
written in a strange, piercing tongue
on every tree and morning dream they had ravaged.

Mount Warning

It was the mountain
I was always going to climb –
swore that heat would not tire me,
flowers and snakes could not
poison my hands or feet:
butcherbirds and crows become
omens of good fortune, guides
to an undergrowth track.

Spurred on by the sight
of the mountain, hill after hill
I climbed for a vantage point:
felt the ice of a willow's breath,
touched the fire that does not burn
in a flame-tree's midday leaves.

Its summits clouded in mist
or the end-of-spring fires,
I walked through ploughed fields
to its foothills, chewed
grass and swallowed rainwater,
gauging its height from burnt-out stumps.
Cattle followed like a scattered procession,
pausing at the creek.
                          I returned home
by a different path – plagued by
its shape and my hesitation.

Under the cover of sunset
I opened my door to its shadow –
abysmal at the threshold!
Prayed that winds and rain
might wash it backwards, into
the desert overnight.

Talking to people, trailing
mullet and catfish,
searching creek banks for rainbow-birds
and tortoises – day and night
the mountain haunted me
like a dying parent's curse.

It became the wish
I never made – the child I never had,
promise I was not to keep,
Bible I should never open:
tomorrow's mountain, always there,
to be climbed without loss and fear.

Unsifted by memory from the shallows of a dream
I left the mountain like gold in a stream.

Flying Foxes

With the hot summer rains they came
out of the forest, crying like lost souls
against a December moon that offered

no respite or refuge from the secrets
they carried to unburden themselves from
in the darkness of river gorges –

or clung, to mango and pawpaw,
while stars pierced their tongues
and breezes mercilessly whipped them on

from tree to tree, valley to valley,
as midnight faded slowly into a Hades
of sunlight and the flying foxes

were gone from yet another night,
here, in the season of jagged hail
that stoned down upon flame-tree and poincianas

while people talked of petals flowing like blood
past doorsteps and along the road.
When sheet lightning tore the sky

the same people prayed, closed windows,
turned off lights and waited
tensely until the fury of winds passed

deeper into the mountains – then prepared
meals as if a holocaust was at hand;
though, at evening, children were allowed outside

to imitate the screams of flying foxes – out to where
every tree stood like a Tower of Famine
that stones would always reach.

Bushfires at Kunghur

The fires burned for weeks on end.
In paddocks where they were put out
logs smouldered for days afterwards.
Farmers talked about how long
before there was rain – this wasn't the west,
but north, east of the ranges,
away from flocks of nuisance galahs.

Water tanks were down, banana plantations
dying under a haze of smoke –
sunlight piercing weatherboards and tin roofs;
water being pumped from the creek
and river. Cattle, hand-fed in silence.

This day the lizards were out
in dozens: head up, immobile like an Aztec warrior
with a frilled ornament around its neck,
one would rear up and flee on its back legs
as your approaching wheels broke the dome
of sunlight protecting it.

As evening fell the wind turned west.
Fires dotted the range
like rubies in Persephone's crown –
men returned home, their eyes
darkened by ashes and soil,
cursing fire-breaks and ruined crops.

Little pepper-grey moths flew out of the bushes,
desperate against the cold panes, thirsty for light.

A Last Mile at Uki

Ghosts would have been always welcome
had any strayed from buried worlds –
but nothing more than dead leaves
ever swept into the room that became
a sanctuary for unbanded fears.

Sometimes you prayed, to no one particular
and for no special reason,
but the sound broke whatever silence was heaped up
by echoes of voices that were dreams away.

Sitting on chairs or the foot of a bed
became the onset of a last-mile walk:
hands strayed to colours and words,
but the end was always a puzzle of furniture
and windows that only poetry or madness could justify.
Neither poetry nor madness was justified,
and sleep came finally as a dream of silhouettes
and the thud of trapdoors as a hooded sandman
entered. Angels were attendants in regulation blue,
and from the back of Aries you saw
giant hands playing at taws with agate planets.
Speech blurred fast, vision fading,
and you wondered why it was you being hanged.

Across deserts you walked until sand was grass,
grass became earth and trees were stumps;
skies went from black to ice-blue
and you knew that every book in the world
had been written –
                    awoke to find sleep
had only passed through a five-minute eternity,
and if they gave you a second chance
the best was yet to come.

Second chances did come, third and fourth too,
until it seemed that sleep or death
were the only substitutes for an absence of ghosts –
a gift from hands that tired of games
and reached out for brighter, more distant stars.
But ghosts were always welcome,
especially when the room was swept of dry grass;
(evening fell like a sudden blindfold,
and giant fingers tapped idly at the foot
of a scaffold where attendant angels wore black crepe).

Bellbird

Textures of leaf and patterns of colour
turned upon thought, turned into words;
but words became cliché, insufficient in the slant
of breeze that moved through ferns
and down fields of lupine. Green scales
assumed the geometry of landscape, outlining
parabolas of hibiscus and stars
that peered upwards as white flannel flowers;
became images of mythology somewhere dreamt of
though speech was immediately muted:
rose, from a tangle of thorns and paperbarks,
through columns of Hawkesbury gums,
cleaving foliage, refracted by light;
settling among the leaves of Ygdrasil
from whose roots Thor's anvil-song
showered upwards in the throat of a bird.

The Finches

Rain fell and thunder boomed over the gorges
like cannon fire in an old war movie
when the finches returned to the orange groves.
From where, like echoes of happy words,
had these tiny red brows and beaks flitted in?
We stood on the veranda watching lightning flash
and cows huddling under the mulberry trees:
listened to our words (that were only reassurances
and hopes for lightning not to break over the house), while
they skirted the orange and lemon blooms,
hopping from heads of waratahs and orchids
only to fall and disappear as a little grey sprinkling
of rain into the grass for seeds.

Clouds and echoes broke again during the night:
silver nails of rain hammered the tin roof
and tanks overflowed to a waste of water.
Sleep came easily – as a dream of grey sky
and leaves falling on to a wet ground:
finches scattering upwards for the darkness
of a forest and leaving behind their outcry
against thunder-storms and a slammed door.

Migrant Bachelor

A page of the letter falls to the floor
and he stares at his cracked hands without speaking.
Twenty years of labour and words draw out
his thoughts with fibro and wood,
yet he does not speak. Somehow the news
of a brother's death has come as no surprise –
along with the usual request for money or goods
to be sent via London or the Red Cross.

The letter is put away into a sideboard
and he goes back into his garden.
He, the last of a family separated by the war,
left in a country where language is still strange;
but where factory chimneys and punch-card clocks
ask no proof of speech or human shibboleth.

Somewhere, Between the First Breath and the Last

Somewhere, between the first breath and the last,
you will pause in crowded light or in darkness
along a street of no local colour (as if a hand
withheld you from encroaching air):
estranged, with reality hanging as a threadbare memory,
you stop: become the unknown voice,

the hands, heart and eyes of someone
you have never been, or will never be again
beyond this transient moment of incomprehension
and bewildered acknowledgment.
You ask: but how long this wait, for the answer
to a question that is a turning of thought:

such a movement and displacement of sense
that logic can only mumble out a phrase
about footsteps walking over your grave, and sunlight
or darkness become oblique shades of emptiness:
those borderless contours of space which are neither
skyward nor ground, angular or level.

Yet it passes, like an angel of death
who has erred on that frightful journey –

                                    The brief,
the sudden and terrific impact of identity passes,
and no more the rush of blood, cold and heavy as quicksilver:
only yourself, from outside and deep within, seen
in a frame that holds what is neither mirror nor portrait.

X-ray

for Frank Croll

The hospital gown hangs like a dreaded shroud.
Voices of people long since passed vibrate
in the room that is neither compartment nor cupboard.
Air of cold darkness circulates around your head,
fringing, passing and forgetting each deep-set crevice
where remnants of logic and order arraign you
by drawing closer the distant beacons of warning.

Now the approaching chaos and inversion of eyesight,
breath held fast; ribs and skull tapped, tapped and held
while recording that reflex of ruptured disorder:
implantation before birth along rivers and bays
of domestic and daily habit: weeds and poisonous vines
that grow up to strangle the crimson flower and clutch
the golden suns of the bee's world and the almond's blossom.

Seeds – attended by hands that we trust, watered
by tears whose springs flow inland from the sea – germinate
in darkness on perspiring hands and cold forehead,
warmed by red light flickering, motors whirring.
Sideways and downwards, downwards and sideways
through channels of turquoise and silver water you peer,
but there is no reflection: these, your rivers and bays,

but no reflection or movement along submarine banks:
only a memory of flowers and trees, fruits and warm suns,
mountain forests, cloudless skies and storm clouds –
the touch of turned earth and the coldness of ice.
All this to be catalogued and filed – this, plus cobwebs
and vermin, spawn of marsh frogs and decayed waterlilies.
Then you, dressed and in sunlight, hear click of shutter
and film rolling through caverns of machinery,
touch what is hair, skin and moist eyes;
line up at the cashier's desk and recall one moment

of sweep along a torrent of skyway and rivers:
fears held back, sorrows and ancestors drowned in currents
of fire, interred among willows and asphodels.
All that recorded for someone else's reference.

Sometimes, in a Dream or Thought

Sometimes, in a dream or thought,
(Darkness in half light – there, always
the hand appears, leading on:
descent by stones of moss beside a fountain
running green in a sun that midnight swallowed;
and always the stop, as limestone caves
and willows come into view.
– Thump of heart, the sweat, the bitten lip,
the fear of further sleep).

a voice enters the heart, though the mind
be deaf, and across the terrain
that only scalpels can lay open, an ocean
of symphony invades the flesh:
discolours, poisons the dust of blood,
and breaks the bones that time has ignored.

(The hand withdraws, leaves bow forward
through crystal beams: green into blue,
blue into an ocean of skyway
roaring about your ears. But harsh the cry
of a man asleep, and foul the taste
of stagnant water).

Though you managed to walk on water,
became the voice that your own heart heard,
ignored and insulted, nightly you walk towards sleep
through limestone caves of morning and noon;
and sometimes, in a dream or thought,
arrive at the one horizon where winds
will leave nothing for music to invade:
where the heart's mischief is mirrored

in the eye of a crow, unmoving as time
and deliberate as hatred –

                        there, upon a desert
of colour that is human flesh, no bigger than your palm,
empty but for the cries of scavenger birds,
you arrive among prickly pear and thistles;
and, as eyelids close for a moment's respite,
you swallow the taste of chalk on your tongue:
feel a wind searing the first flesh from the bone –
but as tears burn downwards, neither morning nor words
        will come.

Scarborough Cemetery

Our thoughts, reflecting the fears that we suppressed,
turned our eyes to the road ahead and searched
the arc of bay to comment on fishing boats and weather.
Within a few seconds and words we passed the headstones:
marble and red brickwork that sea winds scourged;
forgot the three people huddled on the sloping headland,
heads bowed, as a drizzle started and stopped,
and dead flowers swept across the ditches like paper scraps.

Miles further back on the highway the sun had reappeared –
a dozen or more reflections on windows that we caught;
but the wind had brought no quick flashes here:
only the spray of a thousand rivers to wash
the thoughts of three people down the graveyards of the
    mind,
to headlands not discovered, over landforms undefined.

Immigrants at Central Station, 1951

It was sad to hear
the train's whistle this morning
at the railway station.
All night it had rained.
The air was crowded
with a dampness that slowly
sank into our thoughts –
but we ate it all:
the silence, the cold, the benevolence
of empty streets.

Time waited anxiously with us
behind upturned collars
and space hemmed us
against each other
like cattle bought for slaughter.

Families stood
with blankets and packed cases –
keeping children by their sides,
watching pigeons
that watched them.

But it was sad to hear
the train's whistle so suddenly –
to the right of our shoulders
like a word of command.
The signal at the platform's end
turned red and dropped
like a guillotine –
cutting us off from the space of eyesight

while time ran ahead
along glistening tracks of steel.

Feliks Skrzynecki

My gentle father
kept pace only with the Joneses
of his own mind's making –
loved his garden like an only child,
spent years walking its perimeter
from sunrise to sleep.
Alert, brisk and silent,
he swept its paths
ten times around the world.

Hands darkened
from cement, fingers with cracks
like the sods he broke,
I often wondered how he existed
on five or six hours' sleep each night –
why his arms didn't fall off
from the soil he turned
and tobacco he rolled.

His Polish friends
always shook hands too violently,
I thought . . . *Feliks Skrzynecki*,
that formal address
I never got used to.
Talking, they reminisced
about farms where paddocks flowered
with corn and wheat,
horses they bred, pigs
they were skilled in slaughtering.
Five years of forced labour in Germany
did not dull the softness of his blue eyes.

I never once heard
him complain of work, the weather
or pain. When twice
they dug cancer out of his foot,
his comment was: 'but I'm alive'.

Growing older, I
remember words he taught me,
remnants of a language
I inherited unknowingly –
the curse that damned
a crew-cut, grey-haired
department clerk
who asked me in dancing-bear grunts:
'Did your father ever attempt to learn English?'

On the back steps of his house,
bordered by golden cypress,
lawns – geraniums younger
than both parents,
my father sits out the evening
with his dog, smoking,
watching stars and street lights come on,
happy as I have never been.

At thirteen,
stumbling over tenses in Caesar's *Gallic War*,
I forgot my first Polish word.
He repeated it so I never forgot.
After that, like a dumb prophet,
watched me pegging my tents
further and further south of Hadrian's Wall.

Aurea Mediocritas

A wire divides
the clouds and grass.
You place a finger
on the rust of a barb –

hold your breath
as catfish rise,
turning from the shallows
of roots and slime.

A blood-bird settles
in the arms of a vine –
blots out the sun
with a turn of its head.

The midday heat
encircles your eyes –
blurs the scenery
that mountains enclose.

Children climb
the banks of a creek –
showering the water
with pebbles and leaves.

Plovers silently
rise from a sand-bar:
fly down a track
where cattle pass.

You place a finger
on the rust of a barb.
A wire divides
the clouds and grass.

St Patrick's College

Impressed by the uniforms
of her employer's sons,
mother enrolled me at St Pat's
with never a thought
to fees and expenses – wanting only
'what was best'.

From the roof
of the secondary school block
Our Lady watched
with outstretched arms,
her face overshadowed by clouds.
Mother crossed herself
as she left me at the office –
said a prayer
for my future intentions.
Under the principal's window
I stuck pine needles
into the motto
on my breast:
Luceat Lux Vestra
I thought was a brand of soap.

For eight years
I walked Strathfield's paths and streets,
played chasings up and down
the station's ten ramps –
caught the 414 bus
like a foreign tourist,
uncertain of my destination
every time I got off.

For eight years
I carried the blue, black and gold

I'd been privileged to wear:
learnt my conjugations
and Christian decorums for homework,
was never too bright at science but good at spelling;
could say The Lord's Prayer
in Latin, all in one breath.

My last day there
Mass was offered up
for our departing intentions,
Our Lady still watching
above, unchanged by eight years' weather.

With closed eyes
I fervently counted
the seventy-eight pages
of my *Venite Adoremus*,
saw equations I never understood
rubbed off the blackboard,
voices at bus stops, litanies and hymns
taking the right-hand turn
out of Edgar Street for good;
prayed that Mother would be pleased some day
with what she'd got for her money –
that the darkness around me
wasn't 'for the best'
before I let my light shine.

Ancestors

Who are these shadows
that hang over you in a dream –
the bearded, faceless men
standing shoulder to shoulder?

What secrets
do they whisper into the darkness –
why do their eyes
never close?

Where do they point to
from the circle around you –
to what star
do their footprints lead?

Behind them are
mountains, the sound of a river,
a moonlit plain
of grasses and sand.

Why do they
never speak – how long
is their wait to be?

Why do you wake
as their faces become clearer –
your tongue dry
as caked mud?

From across the plain
where sand and grasses never stir
the wind tastes of blood.

Elegy for Don McLaughlin

An only child also
you were equally spoilt –
taken to both extremes,
Paradise and Inferno;
while parents kept guard
with upraised hands
against vices and year-round chills.

Your voice
a good-luck charm
you sang like Burns wrote poetry –
purely, the accent on love;
at concerts and plays
it drew admiration
as death draws silence.

We raced each other
to school in the mornings;
beginning at opposite ends of the hill
on which St Peter's stands,
swerving and skiting
on our bikes – unafraid
of cars or Sister Brendan's cautions,
laughing, out of breath.
Two fifth grade heroes
chastised before the class –
called 'bold, brazen lads'
for the nth time.

On Berala station
they told me how you died –
with all the 'ifs' and 'buts'
that make Fate
so ominous and unkind:

a stolen car, the head-on smash,
you the only one
not to survive.
A girl in a yellow dress
held a transistor
to the wind:
        the Stones
thumped out *The Last Time*
as our train
came noisily in.

I wondered
how dark the night had been,
if any song
had come to mind?

In those morning runs
you always beat me up the hill.
Younger by two years
I was fifteen when you died –
old enough for self-esteem
and showing I wouldn't cry.
Now, on the same road,
I catch up to you
without even having to try.

from A Part of the Air I Breathe
for Judith

1 CONCEPTION

At last
you have come – into the night
and fog that blankets
our house:
like an expected visitor
that failed to arrive
at a promised time.

We stop
looking at clocks –
keep on tearing off
months from
a calendar.

Somewhere
in your fluid darkness
you have become
a part of the air
I breathe –
of the sunlight
you will never grasp:
the dreams
that will confound you
like a jig-saw puzzle
that always has
a missing piece.

Already
there is a weight
upon your unformed shoulders –
the pull and grind
of ancient tides.

The world
is waiting like
a fairytale witch –
her hand
dipped in a bag
full of bones
and gold pieces.

2 NIGHT CALL

Awakened by
your cries
we stumble
from our dreams –

one, two
or three times a night,
lost for direction
as we tread the darkness
towards you,

not knowing
whether pain or hunger
has opened
your eyes to the cold.

Even
without light
you know us
by our voices –
the touch
and warmth of hands:
by echoes
that carry
like a message
through the house.

In my arms
you turn
like a shy, hooded animal
burrowing
into the ground –

frantic, trembling,
as if a net
dragged
at your heels:

Thursday's child –
born in autumn
out of mist and rain,
far to go
and one life
to get there –

but surviving, so far,
and now winter
in the making.

How far
will you go from us
before learning
of dreams
more bitter
than the waking?

10 Mary Street

For nineteen years
we departed
each morning, shut the house
like a well-oiled lock,
hid the key
under a rusty bucket:
to school and work –
over that still too-narrow bridge,
around the factory
that was always burning down.

Back at 5 pm
from the polite hum-drum
of washing clothes
and laying sewerage pipes,
my parents watered
plants – grew potatoes
and rows of sweet corn:
tended roses and camellias
like adopted children.
Home from school earlier
I'd ravage the backyard garden
like a hungry bird –
until, bursting at the seams
of my little blue
St Patrick's College cap,
I'd swear to stay off
strawberries and peas forever.

The house stands
in its china-blue coat –
with paint guaranteed
for another ten years.
Lawns grow across

dug-up beds of
spinach, carrots and tomato.
(The whole block
has been gazetted for industry).

For nineteen years
we lived together –
kept pre-war Europe alive
with photographs and letters,
heated discussions
and embracing gestures:
visitors that ate
kielbasa, salt herrings
and rye bread, drank
raw vodka or cherry brandy
and smoked like
a dozen Puffing Billies.

Naturalised more
than a decade ago
we became citizens of the soil
that was feeding us –
inheritors of a key
that'll open no house
when this one is pulled down.

Devil Fish

A rat-trap mouth, skinless,
each bone a grasshopper's leg –
eyes like portholes we can't look into
from anywhere on zones of palm or ice.

Avoiding sun, catgut and nets to entice,
it swims under heaven's feet and ours.

Rising from black-out caverns of green foam,
leopard-spotted like bullet holes;
ignorant of storms washed up in cowrie shells
it survives an arc of rainbows and flying fish.

Dumb with purpose
it wanders the floor of a lantern world:
celluloid eyes rolling in a head
that is a bone of compasses, hinged to all direction.

A side-on profile is the kneeling angel,
streamlined by tail fins – folded small wings
in prayer,
            but never to watch stars burning like coals
above pits of darkness we shall never climb.

Exiled from a pock-marked sun
it follows its namesake from host to host
while prey falls like manna through a bottomless jaw.

Cattle

With their boxing-glove muzzles
they will stand in your path, heads lowered,
or run stumbling through bracken
and creeks for no reason,
the grass alive with their fear.

Their bodies heavy
with milk and beef – awkward
as felled timber, they live
herded by dogs and whips,
by our curses and impatience.

In downpours and mists
they stand like mute sentinels – immobile
with solemn, wide-open eyes,
staring through hills and fences.

At night they bellow
across paddocks and gullies,
wake us from sleep and reassure us
of our dreams and homestead.

Branded with fire
they have plodded through
grass, mud and water for centuries –
leaving, across continents,
a cleft print

that Humankind will decipher
as an omen of its final hunger.

Carpe Diem

Among the rainflowers
robins sing at first light –
in patches of mist
that hang over a garden:

yellowbreasts and greyheads
perched sideways on stems –
piping to each other,
at play on foxgloves and lupines.

A wagtail swoops down
from the roadside gums –
watches sparrows feed
on grain that was spilt.

Cows have gathered
under a mulberry tree –
silently wait for
someone to come out.

A woman will walk
through the garden,
bucket and stool in hand –
be met by a pair of dogs:

she will bypass
robins, wagtail and sparrows –
walk down a track
that sunrise later follows.

The Birth of a Son

for Andrew

'The birth of a son
should prompt you to write a poem,'
a friend told me
last month over the phone.

I sat and thought,
read a newspaper –
walked around the house alone,
picked dead leaves
off the umbrella-tree.
Still no poem came.

The baby cried
and the house grew larger
with clothes and pram,
toys, bunny-rugs – headaches
that arrived without notice
(doors and windows were left open
but they were always
reluctant to go).

Still no poem.
Only at night the sound
of breathing
                    and footsteps
that are still to come –
hands that have no weight to carry
across a threshold
he already owns.

I think of my father
and the house he lives in –
the land that I came from
and have never known.

My friend's suggestion strikes
like sharpened stones
at night in the darkness

when I speak to my bones.

Diamond Snake

Taken from your keeper's bag
you lie coiled along my arm,
tongue flicking at a kerosene lamp
and moths that night released.

He tells me you are harmless.
Nodding, I disbelieve.

The crack of a branch
and you turn at the moon – stabbing
the darkness I cannot touch.
My arm caressed by a stream of cold water
I wait for you to fall off.

To forget you I look
at the ground – piling shreds
of leaves on to a piece of glass.
The men have stopped dealing cards.
Night has camped itself around us.

With you staring away from me
I turn towards the hut,
watching, from the corner of my eyes
your skin:
        and a thousand tiny fires
burning in the prisms of your scales.

Gleaming like a scythe
you sweep and cut through shadows of grass.
Each time, face-on,
I see your eyes like stains of water
on the pages of a book
I must find and read.

Crossing the Red Sea

1

Many slept on deck
because of the day's heat
or to watch a sunset
they would never see again –
stretched out on blankets and pillows
against cabins and rails:
shirtless, in shorts, barefooted,
themselves a landscape
of milk-white flesh
on a scoured and polished deck.

Voices left their caves
and silence fell from its shackles,
memories strayed
from behind sunken eyes
to look for shorelines –
peaks of mountains and green rivers
that shared their secrets
with storms and exiles.

2

1949, and the war
now four years dead –
neither masters nor slaves
as we crossed a sea
and looked at red banners
that Time was hoisting
in mock salute.

3

Patches and shreds
of dialogue
hung from fingertips

and unshaven faces –
offering themselves
as a respite
from the interruption
of passing waves.

'I remember a field
of red poppies, once behind the forest
when the full moon rose.'

'Blood
leaves similar dark stains –
when it runs for a long time
on stones or rusted iron.'

(And the sea's breath
touched the eyes
of another Lazarus
who was saying a prayer
in Thanksgiving
for miracles).

4
All night
the kindness
of the sea continued –
breaking into
walled-up griefs
that men had sworn
would never be disclosed,
accepting outflung denunciations
with a calmness
that brought a reminder
of people listening to requiems,
pine trees whispering
against a stone wall in the breeze;
or a trembling voice

that sang at the rails
when the ship first sailed
from the sorrow
of northern wars.

     5
Daybreak took away
the magic of dreams,
fragments of apparitions
that became
more tangible than words –
echoes and reflections
of the trust
that men had bartered
for silence.

Had we talked
of death
perhaps something
more than time
would have been lost.

But the gestures
of darkness and starlight
kept our minds
away from the finalities
of surrender –
as they beckoned towards
a blood-rimmed horizon
beyond whose waters
the Equator
was still to be crossed.

Leaving Home

My first country appointment
was the last thing we expected –
three of us, caught unaware
by ignorance and faith:
our dull-witted, frog-mouthed obedience
to the letter of the law.

Counting door handles, ringing telephones
and office boys with denture smiles,
I waited three hours
for a two-minute interview;
watching myself outside in the rain,
my severed head under one arm,
body upright – best white shirt and tie –
a black suit to outdo
the Pallbearer of the Year!
A red-and-white sign at my feet:
'Cabbages for Sale.'
The fiddler from Chagall's village
was inviting me to dance.

The man behind the desk
never once looked me in the eyes –
his face the back of my application papers.
Hawk-nosed, crew-cut, with
a *Tally-Ho* paper skin,
he was the millionth person
who couldn't pronounce my name.
No more, no less,
the verdict came next day by phone:
'You must go.'

We packed the car
like a war-time train – clothes,
books, records, the poems
I'd started writing;
said goodbye so quickly
I forgot for a moment where I was going.

Three hundred miles
up the New England Highway, I stopped;
unloaded my bags for the night;
swore that Head Office
would not see my face again
unless I became my own Scipio Africanus . . .
dreamt of three headless crows
flying in a room
whose rooms were silently burning.
Bald, toothless faces
stood at a window, laughing in the rain,
clapping to a fiddle's music –
their naked, hairless bodies
the colour of sour milk.

Narwhal

Hedges of pack-ice
line the forest where it grazes
on thorns of cuttlefish.

Auroras of sheet-light
spray it with arrows
alongside paddocks of snow and moss.

Whistling and bellowing to itself,
it wanders through towers
of glaciers, trumpeting:
a herald to days without beginnings or end.

Tapestries of lichen
growing black and green, are a scrollwork
it never ceases to weave –
diving over palisades of light
to straits and channels of pasture.

Harpooned or shot,
a legend dies in the Middle Ages –
unicorns vanish on matted floes
through squalls of mist that equators draw.

A scapegoat of reason
it roams in tribes
over Arctic shelves and ridges,
thrusting an ivory blade
at wings of sunlight that follow like a hawk.

Migrant Hostel
Parkes, 1949–51

No one kept count
of all the comings and goings –
arrivals of newcomers
in busloads from the station,
sudden departures from adjoining blocks
that left us wondering
who would be coming next.

Nationalities sought
each other out instinctively –
like a homing pigeon
circling to get its bearings;
years and place-names
recognised by accents,
partitioned off at night
by memories of hunger and hate.

For over two years
we lived like birds of passage –
always sensing a change
in the weather:
unaware of the season
whose track we would follow.

A barrier at the main gate
sealed off the highway
from our doorstep –
as it rose and fell like a finger
pointed in reprimand or shame;
and daily we passed
underneath or alongside it –
needing its sanction
to pass in and out of lives
that had only begun
or were dying.

Chronic Ward
after reading Ken Kesey's One Flew Over the Cuckoo's Nest

Mostly we talk about
the past and how we got here –
where one's born
and why people must die in beds,
how the grass never wears out
with all the short cuts
the moon takes across our eyes
in waking and sleep.

At the state's expense
or our mercy's appeasement –
two, three, six or ten times a stay
we enact the mirror scene
or doctor, visitor and each other:
relive the bathtub drama,
the slip-knot confusion
and oven-door mistakes
before breakfast, lunch or dinner.

Sometimes one of us
makes it – sees Buddha
or Jesus Christ
under their respective, flowering trees
and reports to the others:
all's well with angels; and hell's
not so frightening either –
speaks on the reliability
of x-rays, lumbar punctures
and lobotomised skulls.

We tread the carpet
of our shadows' patterns
like playing a game of stepping on cracks –
day and night, as we talk ourselves into sleep:

every time someone falters,
slips or dies in mid-air
we count to ten before taking a breath –
our voices catching up with us

somewhere between
the night's waking and tomorrow's other death.

Still-born

How cold
was the darkness
that shrouded you –
left you in silence
before silence was known,
closed your eyes
and bowed your head,
dove-like, unmoving?

How gentle
were the hands
that brought you into light –
held you from
expected promises,
turning you swiftly
away from your mother?

How loud
was the cry
you never heard –
that tore from the shallows of bone
like a fish, desperate,
half-dead for air?

How long
were the dreams
that preceded your coming?
Nights of waking
and burnt-out patience
you will never know?

Where will
they go to – the man
and woman who lay claim to you,
speaking the name
by which you will be known?

Flower Garden

1

My parents' garden
always seemed
too full of flowers!
Gardenias, cyclamens, irises,
jasmine, carnations
and roses – a host
of royal names
I could never remember.

Visitors came
and left with bouquets
to shoulder-height –
like pilgrims setting out
for a street
of wayside shrines.

Eventually
the upkeep grew into
a burden:
three-quarters of the garden
uprooted, burned,
the ashes thrown into
Duck Creek.

2

Back from school
I'd sit cross-legged
among the rows,
my blue cap lost
in a maze of colour –
catching ants, dropping caterpillars
into half-open buds,
teasing bees
with a flicking handkerchief.

3

Promising
not to pick flowers
I left briskly
for school in the mornings –
a spring-and-summer madness
that nobody
ever explained.

A snapdragon
in my left-hand coat pocket:
the talisman
I wouldn't part with
until it withered
into red or purple dust.

4

I said nothing
when the garden lost
its flowers –
Time wielding a scythe
in whose path
we had to follow.
The snapdragons
were first to go.

Heritage

There will always be
a face that you never see –
that falls into shadow
at every sunset.

A hundred fingers
will always point at you
from the mirror
in a drop of rain.

You will stir
the depths of every pool
you find – drop pebbles,
pull out pebbles.

Trying to pray
you will imagine God beside you
on the raw earth
of a dug grave.

There will be
no God – devil, father or mother
looking back
from the bottom of a pool.

Not even among
poisoned roots and grassblades
will the splash of rain
grow louder or faint.

The eyes of your child
remind you of water and stone –
it is the answer to a question
that no one will ever ask.

Appointment: north-west

At Jeogla I heard
the mountains tremble,
saw trees shed their leaves
as a storm approached:
heard the wind speak out
from under stones,
watching clouds hang motionless
over dogs and cattle.

It was the country
of frosts and rain, bleak drizzles
that turned walls damp.
Rainbows grew
from the pond in our garden –
covered the Big Hill
in a waterfall of mist.

In summer the hills
ran green with sheep, willows
along creeks
and rider-less horses.

Winter turned
a blind eye to hands,
left its cracks on lips
and knuckles.
At first you checked thermometers
regularly, like a heartbeat –
then learnt about weather
from the colours of a tree.

There you become
the movement of silences,
listen to yourself

talking to magpies and crows –
spend whole afternoons
sitting on the edge of a dam
watching the faces
of dragonflies and geese.

Through drifts
of evening snow
voices call from gullies.
A gate or fence-post answers back.
Dreams crackle in chimneys
blacker than night.

People turn towards
the hills for words – hunt kangaroos
to show visitors
they don't stay home at night:
withdraw to themselves,
talking of dingo baits –
how tanks and pipes
stand up to the cold.

Deserted houses
crowd stones on the track
of a closed-down school and sawmill.
Blackberry bushes
hide lizards and snakes
that watch from
roofs of rusted sheet-iron.

There you look
for early sunsets –
an oncoming trail of dust
along the road,
a stranger or friend that passes.
Your own voice listening
to the whisper of leaves –

as though a mother or father
was speaking to caution.

Leaving each time
was a promise to return,
to settle among hills
that could hide you forever –
knowing time was a crow
you'd never snare,
or the axe that wouldn't rust
in its block on the woodheap.

A Drive in the Country

At Blue Hole
I stood by the water's edge
and watched how swallows swam
through the air –
wild ducks moving away
in the weeds
to their nests in the hollows
of blackberries and reeds.

I stood on a rock
by the roots of a willow –
saw how leaves
bent their ears to the ground.
Gum trees shed
their bark to the wind
and she-oaks dipped their hands
in the shallows.

A chain and rope
hung down from a tree –
over the water for children to swing from.
And I thought of a gallows
to which dead men return
at noon or in darkness
to wait for a crowd.

And still I kept looking
back to the road –
away from Blue Hole
and the miles yet to go:
thinking of the room
where an alarm clock was set
and tomorrow already there.

But only the soft call
of swallows and wild ducks
replied to my thoughts
through the streamers
of blue light.

I spoke to myself
like a man who is dying
and walks away from a road
that runs only one way.

Widowed

Hardly a day passes
that she doesn't work
in her garden – pruning and weeding
on bended knees,
watching the dance of bees
in clumps of lantana
overgrowing her paths.

She pauses longest
among the roses – fingering
petals and buds
as if they were the hem
of a wedding or christening dress –
shyly, almost reluctantly.

Again and again
she returns to a hedge
or vine – stands
as though waiting
for something to happen.

Kneeling on leaves
she won't burn,
on decayed rain
that has turned to moss,
she tends to violets and marigolds –
her dress gathered about her
like a garment of ceremony:
her face overshadowed
by a hat that summer can't pierce,
her future entangled
among thorns and evergreens.

Outside the Delivery Room

They have given me
a green coat
that ties up at the back –
straightjacket and bib
in which to dress my emotions –
my footsteps
clattering up the stairs
because I wouldn't
wait for the lift.

The telephone message
still crackles
in my head – every inch
of five or six miles;
the doctor's voice
imbued with a calmness
that makes me
think of ether
and bright lights.

I didn't even
stop to buy flowers –
card or fruit
to decorate my hands.
Thrilled and
afraid, I raced
April's weather along
the highway – imagining
I was a piece of paper
blown by chance
into the hospital grounds.

What shall
I say – 'Well done'

or speak of love?
Make promises?
The nurse tells me
I can go in.
Hurriedly, I stretch
out my arms,
push open the swinging doors –
as if I suddenly
realised where I was
and had to find
                    my way
out of a labyrinth.

Kornelia Woloszczuk

Her face
betrays the darkness of storms,
winds that alter
the outline of a coast –
eyes to outstare
the face of the waters:
as if hands
were dragging
the depths of a swamp
in search
of her lost son.

Being
her only child,
where did I go wrong –
not knowing
the cave of silence
in which
she outwaited
tides of absence, seas
of loneliness
that lapped her dress
like a prayerwheel,
confined to the centre
of a wasteland
on her palms?

In springtime
she walks beside
a river, pointing out
how water destroys images
that reflect eternity:
grassblades, leaves, flowers –
at whose roots

a fire burns
when a man forsakes
his wife and child.
Her feet
make no imprint
upon the grass
she treads.

Walking
behind her
I listen for birdcalls,
look at breaking water
with every fish in air –
nervous, uncertain
of distances and colours
we pass through.
A dream, she says,
is the path from God:
a faith to cherish
what you inherit
at birth – sustain the winds
on which prophets spoke
across seas
and ruins of hills.
All is sacrificed
for the sake of children
who forget you
before you are dead –
but, remember,
'Having only one child
is like having
one eye in your head.'

Postcard

1

A postcard sent by a friend
haunts me
since its arrival –
Warsaw: Panorama of the Old Town.
He requests I show it
to my parents.

Red buses on a bridge
emerging from a corner –
high-rise flats and something
like a park borders
the river with its concrete pylons.
The sky's the brightest shade.

2

Warsaw, Old Town,
I never knew you
except in the third person –
great city
that bombs destroyed,
its people massacred
or exiled – you survived
in the minds
of a dying generation
half a world away.
They shelter you
and defend the patterns
of your remaking,
condemn your politics,
cherish your religion
and drink to freedom
under the White Eagle's flag.

For the moment,
I repeat, I never knew you,
let me be.
I've seen red buses
elsewhere
and all rivers have
an obstinate glare.
My father
will be proud
of your domes and towers,
my mother
will speak of her
beloved Ukraine.
What's my choice
to be?

I can give you
the recognition
of eyesight and praise.
What more
do you want
besides
the gift of despair?

3
I stare
at the photograph
and refuse to answer
the voices
of red gables
and a cloudless sky.

On the river's bank
a lone tree
whispers:
'We will meet
before you die.'

FROM *The Aviary* 1978

Parents

They stand at the gate
like a part of the garden itself –
waving through shadows
already between us;
the last words spoken
five minutes ago
in the silence of an empty garage.

A summer morning
filled with irretrievable regrets,
roses in blooms,
the scent of jasmine –
a myriad of lambent thoughts
that shatter
as I turn and face the windscreen:

embedding themselves
in momentary brilliance
along veins
and trembling nerve-ends.

Amid the fragments of air and light
the road begins to curve
like a question mark
laid down between us forever.

Old Hostel Site

Lime Kilns Road, Bathurst

The biggest surprise
comes in finding the expected
after an absence
of twenty-seven years –
barbed wire, broken fences,
bare hills strewn
with decaying logs.

Two wooden barracks
and one tin hut
remain like immense souvenirs
of a war the signpost
doesn't point to.

For a whole lifetime
my parents talked of this hostel
where we first came to
in Australia –
here, at the edge
of a cleared forest and its creek,
beside the main road
that led to work
and the strange hills further north.

Twenty-seven years crowd
into the space of what's become
three storage sheds
on a farmer's property –
among machinery, horsefloats, fodder;
packed beneath the rafters
like remnants
of unclaimed baggage.
I shade my eyes
from the glare of corrugated iron,

bleached wood and wired glass –
recognising the syllables of wind and water
as they wash over
the accents of old sights.

Cattle allow my intrusion
across the grid
where a willy-wagtail breaks into song.

Barking dogs rip at air
and the illusions
of rediscovery I'd brought.

Apple Orchard

Light fills the boughs
with a green burden –
pierces each leaf
with slivers of gold,

warms the groves
and riverside flats –
the flesh of hyacinths
and spirals of roses;

a springtime gust
flooding the valley,
across tracks
of cattle and men –

cicada, whipbird,
wren, king parrots:
whose songs rise
over the homestead.

A farmer and his wife
speak of the picking –
how the crop bursts
in clusters of white;

while the sun
burns into their eyes
like a wound –
and the black snake,

watching, sinks
on to a lower ledge
of sandstone
blackened by fire –

awaiting the birth
of a five-pointed star
in the heart
of every blossom.

Per Omnia Saecula Saeculorum

i.m. James McAuley

Thirty years and the night's
still black, day alternates between
gold and darkening blues –
and still no horizon
that doesn't reflect the boundaries
of space in a single word.

You learn to count
by ones and twos, decades, centuries –
the insignificant symbols
that comprise your every day:
front gate, bus stop, the local school,
a row of trees you pass through.

Thirty years and you learn
to bestow a name upon
order and the appearance of things –
to view each scene as though
it were sometimes the last:
a blend of colours, the joy in a laugh.

And still you draw circles
in the air, on stone and wet sand –
accepting a scintillant pattern
of stars as though it were
God's own hand –
                              appeased, until,
passing a playground

the youngest voice catches
in your mind like a branch –
snags at a thought
that won't leave you alone:
reminds you of days lying beneath
the soil of flesh and bone.

The Goldfish

The pond fills with a green light
that breaks up
whenever the fish rise,

reflects a pattern of scales
or faces that peer down
with questions and replies.

The fish surface and swarm
to where food
is dropped – telescope eyes,

veil tails, mouths agape
among ripples and bursts of water:
snap, frantic

in their hunger and speed
as if a hand
scooped at their lives.

They gulp and tear
at pieces of bread, stare back
with sullen, opaque looks –

motionless, fins and tails
trailing like scarves
caught in the stems of lilies:

globular bodies,
comets, goggle-eyed –
nudging against human presences

with bullet-like heads
and sides that heave
like a bellows.

Stan Kostka

In his last years
he was always the unexpected guest –
arriving at my parents' home
on Sunday afternoons,
believing, that a drink with friends
should start
the working week.

For hours the conversation
followed them
around the house and garden:
Poland, the War,
how families became scattered over the world –
Australia's changes in twenty years;
and even a slice of rye bread
can seem too heavy
when you think you've come
far enough in life.

Close by
his wife regarded the sky
more casually –
then cautioned against staying
too long in the rain.

At his funeral
the priest spoke of homelands
and possessions –
what a man gains
when he loses his children.

I thought it was almost a eulogy –
remembering how he laughed
whenever the talk

was threatened by rain or silence;
and once, winking,
lifted his glass in a toast:
'To the next five days
of our new-found lives which,
like a crowded ship,
go down
very, very slowly.'

Sportsfield at Milperra

A week after the floods
I went down to the river –
between the bridge
and council tip, the playing fields
still under water.

Footprints and wheels ruts
formed countless maps
beneath the black eyes of frogs
and climbing snails –
while the bruised reflection
of cloudbanks
drifted around crests
of debris and grey sand.

Waterbirds fed
among paperbarks and banksias –
like river-attendants
dressed in white and black:
ibis, plover, gulls
and pelican,
                    undisturbed
by my presence
or the city's hurried Sunday.

It seemed
as if all time had finally ended
by this lone stretch
of bushland and flattened grass;
or, in isolation, once more
was starting to evolve –
while birds appeased
a winter's hunger
and their wing spans filled

the spaces between
branches and a daylight moon:

and my own life ebbed
like receding water
beneath a set of empty goal posts,
among black strands
of floating weed,
into a sloping labyrinth of tracks
whose exit was the river.

The Hired Lady's Son

His mother's eyes
never left his mind
whenever she was out of sight –
and the house absorbed her presence
into its rooms, punctually, one by one.

Dutiful, like
a wooden-headed puppet,
he obliged the formal rules of courtesy
by keeping out of 'madam's' way:

who sat him
in the sandstone garden
beneath a staghorn's greening arms –
and, with an eloquent silence,
gave him *The Sydney Morning Herald* to read
and occupy himself all day.

Sunshine poured
through bay-windows, ricochetted off
polished silver, rosewood, mosaics of stained glass;
suspended dust motes
in the lacquered piano room
watched his face as he quickly passed.

Eventually, butterflies
ceased to tease him with their circling tongues;
caterpillars journeyed across his sandals,
stalks of irises his fingers gave –
and the patterns that he traced in soil
became a track for each ant's load.

Only the newspaper
from which he was learning to read

never lost the origins of its purpose, its
Strathfield homeland tongue;
yellowed, by late afternoon ('Time, dear, to go home') –
parched, by that summer's day,
from the message it was meant to impart.

Good Friday Morning

Now the mind awaits Calvary,
confronts the depths
to which a soul will fall –
accepts the burden of a three-hour death,
The Stations of the Cross.

Eyes close upon
a crown of thorns, the scourge,
a dying thief's humble plea:
the ignominy of a cross at sunset
overlooking the Holy Land.

Now Gethsemane lies beyond
reach, the defiance of a sirocco wind –
Peter's sword, the act of Judas,
like grass blades dropped forgetfully
into an ocean stream.

Stained glass echoes the voice
of psalms: Isaiah, Exodus, Gospel of St John –
water and blood, symbol and substance
of baptism, redemption.

Now the mind puts aside
its words, genuflects on the silence of floors –
sinner's guilt and the innocent child
kneeling side by side to proclaim
a faith: the mystery of forgiveness.

Tabernacle empty, altar stripped bare,
sanctuary lamp extinguished,
a crucifix veiled until the afternoon –
church doors opened to admit the light
upon a vigil that has no ending.

Arrival from Austria

Italy, 1949

All morning we walked
along a street of rain,
under leafless trees and singing wires –
driven forward by a wind
at our backs,
relentlessly, like a voice of conscience.

Walls of houses
watched our progress –
spoke nothing, and continued to stare,
while packs of clouds
rolled overhead and thunder
rumbled in the distance.

A storm passed
the previous week
on a station by a forest of pines –
where aeroplanes lay broken
like giant toys
carved from fragile wood.

But the wind dispersed it all –
pine trees, windows,
rail tracks, the landscape
of a brooding storm;
brought us within sight
of a black ship
moored to a dock in the distance –
as rain continued
to spatter our faces and hands
in drops
        that ran off
like hieroglyphics.

My Father's Birthday

His grandchildren
run out to greet him, carrying
Polish 'Happy Birthday' phrases
from a song
I've tried to teach them:
'*Sto lat, sto lat. Sto lat*, Dziadzia.'
Then turn, applaud
each other's efforts.
Stooping, he laughs,
returns their kisses.

I cannot bring myself
to think of him
as a 'septuagenarian' –
as if something
harsh and abrasive
rubbed against sensibilities
I didn't want offended,

or simply
that I've grown up
unprepared
to face a future
that will not include
his physical presence
permanently.

(The children starting to remember
more and more
of the song . . .)

There are no candles
on his cake;
yet I pray to the God

he believes in
that even seventy eternities
will never extinguish
whatever fire's burning in him

but gently permit to kindle.

A Bush Walk at Jeogla

Once I came
to a creek in the hills,
under a ridge of crumbling stones –
and stood at the edge by a granite boulder
to rest for a moment and watch the sun.

Dragonflies and beetles
skimmed the surface like targets of polished steel –
while my tracks ran through a tangle of grass,
from the gullies where I wandered
across shallows of lichens and weeds.

The sun hung
like a ringed furnace above the tallest trees –
as if I hadn't noticed it before,
pouring its stream of quicksilver yellow
against the water's speech.

And the glare
threw back the colour of sky,
a pattern of clouds and transparent wings –
while my shadow fell like a cape
across the eroded ridge.

The sun continued
to burn through shades,
surface of water and beetles' wings –
a will to get up and resume my way
along a different path than the one I came.

I sat on the boulder
and rested longer than I wished –
while Time ran past like water and sunlight shattered
the course of a day that was set
and is still unfinished.

Styx River (2)

A river enclosed by walls
of leaf, tangles of thorn
and impassable blossoms –
ironbark, bloodwood, blackbutt trees
that sank their roots through earth's granite.

A year of travelling to its edge
and watching trout glide through dark shallows –
never questioning the length
of the track on which I stood
or where it ended altogether;

never daring to step across
and break the surface of a sunken world –
whose waters were only a tributary
of a wider, deeper river.

Et Verbum Caro Factum Est

You trace the lifeline
of a scarlet petal
along a stem that burns
with the Arctic's green –

find, among stones
and transparent shells,
the quelled fire of dead moons
struck by gods unseen.

You reach out to touch
the shadow of a bird,
a flight of anger that passes
in you like shaken leaves –

yet nothing's said:
one, two, ten times a day
of the peace that descends upon you
with a watercolour ease.

You count the pages
of a waterstained text,
reread the stories
of Gilgamesh and Ulysses –

glimpse the vision
of a sorrowful angel
at the gates of a garden
overshadowed by voices.

And still you dream
of a point beyond space
where archives no longer exist,
flowers grow without rain.

Over the shadow
of a cross you stand –
touch the stem of a flowering rose
and bleed, but feel no pain.

Wśród Nocnej Ciszy

Three hours before midnight
and already the words of a hymn
fill the house
with their grave tones –
a melody in the form
of a solemn polonaise that affirms
the year's turning.

The table set, food, wine,
wrapped gifts beneath
a miniature tree –
outside, a darkness on red brick
begins to match the lines
on faces and hands.

I stand on the veranda
and listen to a mingling of voices –
the refrain that repeats
its yearly message
through a translation of custom and traditions:
'In the Still of the Night',
'Dans le Calme de la Nuit' . . .
Crickets and beetles
exchange their own Christmas manifesto
with soil and the grass's damp.

Like a slow running of water
the charms of folk history
assume the shape of a chorale piece –
rising, swell to pour out
a defeat of passions,
surge to a point
three hours ahead of time
beyond which midnight
and feast days exist as one.

And one by one
chairs are filled, candles lit
around a vase of red roses –
glasses raised in a toast
to the message of The Word;
while children laugh
at new delights
and
        bread and salt remain
to be gathered from the table.

Sailing to Australia
1949

1

Tired, embittered,
wary of each other –
like men whose death sentences
have been commuted,
they turned their faces
from a shore
none of them could forget.

2

Leaving from
a Displaced Persons' Camp
in Germany,
we travelled south
by train into Italy.

Coming through Austria
I remember
walking between carriages,
seeing aeroplanes
lying broken in a forest –
their yellow and black
camouflage
like a butterfly's
torn wings.

3

Through grey mornings
and long afternoons of drizzle
we lay and talked
of graves that nobody
was prepared
to enter –
      argued

about war, disguised nationalities
and the absence of sea birds
for whom we always watched.
And all the time
someone, sooner or later,
remarking:
'Nearly, nearly there.'

Though officially
tagged and photographed
to the satisfaction of braided uniforms
we had no names –
a tattooed number
or the gold fillings in a heart
to be disclosed only
to St Peter at The Gates.

For all it
mattered, where kinship
or affiliations
were concerned, each of us
could have been
an empty bullet shell
or prints left by a scavenger bird
around a piece of bone.
Each face became
a set of facts –
a situation
to be associated with
only while the voyage lasted.

4
Even the worst weather
became an ally
to whom confidences and sorrows
were readily confided –
disinherited, self-exiled,

homeless
as a river without banks,
people turned their backs and minds
upon the fallen godhead
of a country's majesty,
quietly embracing the comfort
in every drop of salt
that crystallised into manna
on their tongues and in their eyes;
often, waiting until
the moon appeared
like a promised sign –
and the ship might leave the water
to a Castle of Dreams
in the clouds –
before they went to sleep.

5

On arrival,
a great uneasiness
filled the ship –
unspoken, misunderstood,
as a Union Jack
was hung
across the landing dock.

With the solemnity
of a basking sea lion
a government interpreter
held a loudspeaker at arm's length –
telling us, in
his own broken accents,
why we should feel proud
to have arrived,
without mishap, in Australia,
on Armistice Day.

The Aviary

1

He took the packing cases
apart, measured the boards, planed, sawed;
put it all together
with nails and galvanised wire.
From discarded timber at a local factory –
a cage for colours, song, flight.

With a pride that hoped to equal his skills
I supplied the birds –
selecting pairs for their beauty,
hardiness, temperaments
to survive with each other.

2

Now we stand at a distance
to watch their circlings, rapid leaps of flight –
the endless play of light on feathers;
listen to the tiny
trumpet-like calls that interrupt our conversation
and carry beyond the backyard.

3

In the evenings,
after my father's gone, I look inside
the aviary and see
the vanishing point of our lives –
unlike plumage, perfections we never owned,
birds settled, perches quiet.
Only a hammering of nails and wood
being sawn fills the darkness with wounds
like the echoes of an old despair.
Four decades and the craft of an other age away
my father is always there.

Cockatoos at Summer Hill

It was wrong to believe
we owed them nothing for this visit –
beyond the grappling conjectures
why winds and stars
swept their lives off course.

After all, now we had
the constant companionship of intrigue –
spectacular shotgun blasts
that resound only in our bones at night,
scratchy heads and chests
as we hypothesise
how wrinkled and fair their skin must be;
and the lawns strewn with remnants
of corncobs and sunflower seeds
that only attract sparrows and starlings.

Still, who would change it?
Imperial gold crests and white shafts
that decked our winterweeds
with a fabulous luxury;
every glassy-black eye rolling
like a tiny ocean,
distorting our smiles and benevolence –
and the logic of harsh, raw cries
that ripped open the monotony
of our ageing, suburban days.

Who would? As we peer over fences
into each other's lives,
on tiptoes, our muscles ache –
each of us,
            clinging to a rotten paling
and an inaudible scream for balance.

The Jeogla Road

I worked by a road
in the New England hills
that ran up from the Oaky Creek –
and held the school
in a bend of stringybarks
and broken granite.

When asked, the locals
pointed out the direction of its end –
beyond the ranges of
the Styx forest: past gorges,
chasms, an abandoned mine,
the flashing cries of mountain lowries.

And their words
reminded me of shadows –
a permanent darkness
in the wind or trees:
as if the road was part of a secret
their lives were sworn to keep.

Only 'coastline' and 'Macleay'
kept all that year
from decomposing like fallen grass –
knowing that people lived
beside sand and water and depended,
also, on the road.

And when it came
time to leave, I stood on the rim
of the road's first crest –
beside the school,
listening to the oncoming dark
and the cries of soldierbirds:

as if to confront
the rising moon or meet a total stranger –
who would then assure me
that the existence of an ocean
was only a myth
and he, himself, a passing spectre.

Black Madonna

Even before
you notice the gash
the skin's pallor
burns like
a sun – invokes
an image of
lit candles,
the whispered breath
of midnight vigils.

The long, melancholy face
turns aside
as if distracted
or bored –
robed in a black cape,
exposing to view
the slashed right cheek:
golden lilies
in a carmine lining.

Her son's right hand
blesses you –
pilgrim, exile
and curiosity seeker:
offering
jewelled secrets
from a casket
he bears –
like a gift proclaimed
and extended.

Together they stand
vulnerable against Time,
Tartar's arrow

or Hussite sabre –
enshrined with
the hues of a partitioned faith,
the permanence
of Częstochowa's
Baroque portals:

while people
stare at the scars
on a face
that neither paint
nor water removes –

whose forked shape
shines between Palestine
and Jasna Góra
like a star

or the barbs
of a future portent.

Returning to Regents Park

1

So the country stay
is over, he said.

                And I will forget
the road's red dust, leaves tinged
with sorrowful mists,
the stone gripping its last drop of moisture
as the fire splits it black –
the cattle's patience, lowing stride,
a sheep's dull stare
through wet grass;
parrots, fish, a thirsting snake,
black swans resting
at the pond's bare edge . . .

2

Across the roofs of three small schools
I looked and tried
to see the world –
three peaks of stained,
corrugated iron
where fear and joy ran off:
down peeling gum trees,
spurs of granite, gullies
of clay and fern-lined quartz –
while stars pinpointed the direction of home
beneath opaque clouds
that bloomed like the flowers of Ygdrasil:

each school with its horse paddock
and neighbours
who recounted local history –
the shy, inquisitive
country folk with calloused hands

and browned skin,
observing the newcomer
whose name they couldn't pronounce.
And I, the stranger
in their homes and gardens,
intruding upon their children's lives
in the noonday presence of lupines and orchids,
camphor laurels, flame-tree, pines
and burning sugar cane.
'How was Mount Warning named?'
Or, 'From where do the flying foxes come?'

Among us all
who was not a stranger,
gathered in winter
at the homestead
on the Styx?
          Wondering
how far south
were parents waking?
Or, looking to find the gate
I dreamed of opening
upon a sea that flowed to the Venusberg:
a childhood's sleep inside
peach-coloured walls, by a veranda
of roses and climber jasmine?

3
Earnest, impassioned, yet calm,
each letter from home
began *drogi* –
filled with words
of patience, advice against getting
the 'flu and insect bites.
Besides 'dear'
it also meant 'roads' –
as every sentence

confronted a path of frost,
a stranger to be met
and welcomed at the school's door.

4

Blunt truths
instilled to children
                              to justify
the monotony of weathered guideposts,
rivers, gorges, hillsides,
farmhouses and paddocks at night,
highways remembered
by their steep descent, slow lanes
and innumerable speed signs:
only to learn
that Time kept up with him
like a giant cloud – even when he was standing still;
and that deceitful friend, Age,
exacting payment every year
in the name of experience or wisdom.

5

Jeogla, Kunghur, Colo Heights,
like strange names
on a postage stamp
    from countries
    that never existed –
exchanged for the sight
of railway lines, cemented gardens
and asphalt playgrounds:
pieces of a daily
jigsaw puzzle that occasionally fit together
as if to form a word –
then, without sound's reach,
                              break up
                              and fade
of their own accord.

from Rookwood Cemetery

1 Russian Orthodox Grave

It stands out
like a piece of coastline –
jagged, unfinished,
slanting to the east:
cut from slabs of pink sandstone
with veins
of cream and white.

Pine tree, barberry,
silver birch
grow on all sides.

'Your son?'
I asked the old couple
bringing water and red flowers
in the rain.

'Grandson,'
the woman replied softly –
as if not to be
overheard.

I looked or their car.
There was none.
The gates at Barker Road yawned
behind them like a chasm –
a sprawl of roofs
and treetops
peering through the white bars.

We spoke
in broken accents.

I looked
at what they carried –
water, flowers, other signs of life.
A white patriarchal cross rose
out of the stone's
heart:

    cutting the air between us
like a broken, upraised knife.

2 IRISH SETTLERS

There's hardly one
that hasn't toppled or begun to crack –
headstone on headstone,
cross smashed against cross:
in the barest, darkest corner
of the cemetery –
stale with dust and the absence
of human speech.

Horses graze in
the grounds of Lidcombe State Hospital
over the fence –
in the same drab inertia
that floats down from a suburban sky.

The magic of green hills
and stone bridges, legends, songs –
an indomitable will to survive
drift behind the stern
of a ship long since forging
through eternity's winds and sleet.

Rose O'Hagan, James Donovan,
Patrick Corcoran
and a hundred other names –
forgotten immigrants from Dublin,
County Clare, Tipperary . . .

Blackberry-canes wrap around them
like green lassoes
of human skin.

And like a distant,
undiscovered harbour, the exit is far
on the other side –
away from the privacy of dead grass
and the darting voices
of silvereyes:

where monuments
disappear quietly from view
under horses' eyes
and the green emblem of a nation's fortunes
lies ploughed beneath
the burden
of cracked slabs and twisted iron.

3 PRESBYTERIAN EPITAPHS

The doctrines of John Calvin
offer no comfort in the presence
of marble slabs,
rusting bolts and bleached stones –
motifs entwined
with roses and vines
beneath a canopy of spring branches.

Spirits from Ayr,
Glasgow, the Shetland Isles
cling to their last words
with a zeal that cracks
the embrace of southern weather –
revealing the proximity of death
in its ageless districts
as a vision of sunlit decay
and blossoming tree-stems.

Who's predestined
for a fate different to this?
Ordained for a light
that reveals only another Darkness?
Echoes of Genesis,
The Psalms, Ecclesiastes, sway
in unison with the wind
and the songs of nameless birds.

Freesias raise
their white trumpets from a shroud
of brown grass;
hibiscus blaze as stained-
glass portals
along a wall of green pines;
moss clings to bark, burial urns,
blackened headstones
in the shape of cathedral spires –
assaulting the visible
language of spring
in tartan shades of Gaelic pride!

Facing the east,
one epitaph overshadows
the hill's slope
with an inscription
common to all faiths:

As for man, his days are as grass;
As a flower of the field so he flourisheth.
For the wind passeth over it, and it is gone;
And the place thereof shall know it no more.

My mind thumbs through a text
of leaves and flowers,
searching for an epitaph
appropriate to my life's end –
wondering in what direction

Calvin's own grave lies:
the birthplace where a soul
is chosen to leave its body –
before stepping out
to embrace the darkness
at the edge of final precepts.

4 COLONIAL GRAVES

Screened by
camphor laurels and hoop pines
their graves stand
like milestones along a disused road –
navigator, merchant, boatswain, carpenter:
the nineteenth-century colonists
whose final harbour came to lie
between a railway line
and a block of suburban factories.

Overgrown with moss,
beliefs and prophecies lie revealed
on wreaths and granite blocks –

Abide in Me, Jesu Mercy,
The Day of the Lord
Cometh as a Thief in the Night.

Above the weeds,
by the road's perimeter,
mourning doves and a kneeling angel
overlook a stormwater channel
and the exhausts of passing cars.

Roses grow wild
in wooden gazebos, over
latticed walls and sandstone floors –
fill the air with scarlet hues
like signs
of imminent danger.

I stand on the edge
of a memorial pool
by a path of lantana and lichens –
listening to a silence
that breathes over water
and the echoes of birdcall:
search for bearings that point to a globe
devoid of Death
and its crumbling symbols –
errors of quest for Identity,
New Lands and Other Religions –
the genealogy of races
reflected in the eyes of water
and the evergreen shades of a laurel's beauty.

Nearby,
in the shape of a marble helm,
the epitaph of a seaman's grave
looks southwards
towards the cemetery's exit:
England Expects
that Every Man Will Do His Duty.

5 MARTYRS' MEMORIAL

The secrets of ferns and river stones
lie behind open gates –
facing the east, a strange collection,
striking the sun and passing faces
with the greyness of its eyes.

Day lends colour to granite.
Night washes the peace with transparent black –
the immense silence
that keeps its motionless vigil
beside a harbour of signposts and names.
Buchenwald, Treblinka, Babi-Yar,
flap like paper blinds
in the minds of a jostling crowd.

Outside, roses open
their mouths to the rain –
camphor laurels grow wide as a church.
Smaller than both,
a bronze plaque commemorates
the dreams of dead children.

Visitors take part
in a theatre performance,
in the midst of asphalt and birds –
enact the light, the voice of clocks,
the thunder of pain
that crumbles bones or a palace.
Freight cars rattling on tracks nearby
are the constant
and daily applause.

6 UKRAINIAN SECTION

I remember letters
from my mother's homeland
every time I stand at the entrance –
the strange, irregular shapes
of a Slavic alphabet
that's perplexed me since
I first began to read!

No purple inks
or soft-grained paper
report news of illness
or comment on the wisdom
of conveying hope –
the hammer and sickle
emblem flying
over three decades
strikes no splinters
on the fingers
of a white picket fence.

Tea-trees, gums and wattles
form a guard of honour
along the short and circular drive –
kerbed and guttered
like a suburban cul-de-sac.
A stone's throw away
railway workshops
form a tapestry
of wires and galvanised iron.

Carved into granite
and marble,
the blind eyes of angels
and outstretched arms of Mary
confront me with questions
that rip at the flesh
of my own inheritance:

the golden Trident
on a field of blue
cracking heaven's geometry
with its strength –
a *bandura's* voice
below The Carpathians
that gloom eastwards
like a mourning wall –
or the steppes of Galicia
throwing their
embroidered hues
between
The Dnepr and the sun.

A mass of history
and statistics
snaps back automatically,
punctuating my blood
with answers in black and white –

culture, religion,
the wealth of industries,
a pillage of destiny and free will –
in a language
I will never have to learn
beside a railway gauge
or at Crimea:

seeing the final address
of my life
written down
in the indelible symbols
of an Alphabet
every human learns to read.

7 POLISH HEADSTONES

No White Eagle hangs
in the air
and no Black Madonna
in a shrine of birches
implores a pilgrim's stare.
On the red-clay slope,
streaked with sand, the Polish headstones
face east and west –
back to back,
as if shunning each other's presence.

A row of prunus,
bottlebrush, palms –
a white chain fence
enclose emblems of belief
and the end of a life's migration:
silver crucifix, rosary beads,
a broken candle –
set behind glass, within niches
of polished granite.

As in life,
the syllables of pronunciation
distinguish their epitaphs –
here, in the western suburbs
of their final rest:
Tu Spoczywa
W Bogu;
Spokój Jego Duszy;
Na zawsze w pamięce.

Again and again
I pause, stumbling
over consonants –
repeating the infinite conjugations
of a verb that suggests
the boundaries
of eternity.

But the headstones
ask nothing about tenses –
the purposes of visits
or yesterday's weather.
Like compasses set in the earth
they point east and west forever
while people come and leave
among them from all sides

only to find they are eventually walking
in the same Direction together.

First Day at School

There is something fairytale
about his little blue cap
under which he sits like an elf
in the back row –
hardly daring to look sideways
as the voice of 'Sir'
strides around the room
in a black cassock:

Inspecting uniforms,
hands, fingernails, school cases –
the strict adherence
to a set of rules
laid down by
discipline and tradition.

Around him
the plaster statues of saints
offer no comfort
from their pedestals:

Jesus, Mary, St Joseph,
St Therese –
as well as the patron saint
of Eire and Strathfield's Irish.

Below him, car horns
and crowding voices
double-park
in Edgar Street.
Mother and fathers
shake the hands of teachers

to whom they've entrusted
their sons' futures.

Thankfully, he passes
the inspection
without a mark
against his appearance –
all the attention and care
his mother put into pressing his clothes
eventually paying off.

At his name
the teacher pauses,
commences to pronounce it
and stops, hesitates for a moment.
The sly flicker of a smile
passes across his eyes.
Tongue-tying himself cleverly
he mispronounces it –
tries and tries again.
Voices laugh. No one objects.
Finally, he asks,
'Tell me, boy, how do you pronounce that?'

The Polish Immigrant

He has grown tired
of the clichéd
pronunciation of his name –
countering
the inadvertent 'How d' yer . . . ?'
that humour
or rudeness asks,

a few vowels
and tooth-grinding consonants
that must be
phonetically rehearsed
alone or at night,

to forestall jibes,
embarrassments, false curiosity –
the wasted time
that a Handbook-and-Timetable
devotee provokes.

Yes, he would argue,
there must be places
in history
where land or heritage
asks no exile
of the children it nourishes
and helps to breed,

where a name's
not laughed at, reviled
or twisted
like some gross truth
or as yet unnamed, imported
European disease.

So, he asks,
Tell me of Strzlecki,
count-turned-explorer –
beside whose name
a creek flows
through the deserts
of South Australia?

Or why a mountain, peaked
with snow,
should resemble a tomb
and be named
Kosciuszko?

Their eyes narrow,
nostrils quaver –
the seconds
between them toll.

Deeply breathing
their mouths open
darkly
and groper-slow.

Night Swim

Stroke upon stroke
he tires himself out from an impulse
that haunts his sinews and bones –
the water's obstinacy yielding
to hands that cleave an escape
into a green darkness that filters in
from the walled-off sea.

Within the perimeters of cliff-side lights,
walkways, jowls of sandstone
profiled on Bilgola's sky –
he cordons himself off
from a day that blurs his eyes
and stings with a salt
no sea dissolves.

A burst of fragmented voices overtakes him,
echoes of distances he crossed in thirty-three years:
birthplace, parents, his two
young children –
a marriage shattering in dissolution
like surf on a virginal
backbone of sand:
landscapes of inheritance
he tears his palms on
as though trying
to peer over a serrated horizon –
admissions of success and failure
nakedly coalescing:
                              momentarily distilled
like a springtime essence

into a single drop of the sea.
Swallow it, he tells himself –
stomach it and learn to swim as never before.
Curse the moon, tides
and people (elements of Change
you cannot flee). Accept the darkness,
abyss between planets –
dome of eternity whose only light has been the stars.

Behind him the water shimmers
like spilled oil
and he heaves himself
on to the green wall.

Discoveries? Of what –
in two lengths of chained-off time?
Hardly worth the hour's drive
from suburbs where he lived
and never once questioned day-to-day purposes,
effects of years on heart and mind.

He laughs at a small mottled crab scuttling sideways
at his feet
(only to fall back into the sea) –
as though he himself
was something
it actually had to fear.

Brown Frog

Squatting
like Buddha among stones
and lilies, its round brown body
the colour of snails –
it glistens with a permanent wetness
of spawning grass and ancient slime.

A puffed-out chest
sucks in night's damp, releases it
like a hollow smack –
undisturbed by
the moon's grave stalking
that floods the yard with ashen light.

Two black pearls
or ebony drops, rising bulbous
over a convex brow –
contrasting with a thin-wire mouth
that patiently waits for night
to descend like a permanent shroud.

Returning with
the briefest plop, a stone
dropped straight into a castle's moat –
surfacing with
                    the stealth of an avenger
and tirelessly begins to summon its mate.

Styx River (3)

A name was borrowed from Greek mythology,
a name of silence, darkness, dread –
put up beside the road to Kempsey
where Jeogla ends and cattle tread.

Crows and currawongs perch on it.
Snakes glide past and disappear behind logs.
Farmers ignore it as they ride past
with bellowing herds and barking dogs.

Below it, far below, water trickles hungrily
through crevices and ledges of stones.
Leaves and bracken swirl in eddies
around granite boulders formed like giant bones.

Follow it through dark ravines,
eucalypt forests and a chasm of primeval sounds –
clefts in a mountain the size of a glacier
in which your sense of direction drowns.

Wildlife will be our only companions,
shadows that fall into silence at your feet –
kangaroo, wallaby, dingo, possum:
black cockatoos that screech if you fall asleep.

Or, better still, pass on.
Forget the river at the bottom of a gorge,
rainbow trout, the mysterious lure of its name
like strange music or a flower's scent –

remember previous visits made to the underworld
and what the return journey meant.

Migrant Centre Site
Orange Road, Parkes

Galahs and crested pigeons
scatter at my intrusion
into the paddock of autumn grasses
where horses continue grazing –
where agaves, pines and oleanders
have been planted like exotic memorials
among native eucalypts.

Climbing over a barbed-wire fence
I discover the remains
of the migrant centre where we lived
on first coming to Australia –
where the lives of three thousand refugees
were started all over again
in row upon row of converted Air Force huts.

Broken slabs of concrete
like baking in the sun –
pieces of brick, steel and fibro
that burrs and thistles have failed to overgrow
even after thirty-three years.
Several unbroken front-door steps
still stand upright and lead nowhere.

Except for what memory recalls
there is nothing to commemorate our arrival –
no plaques, no names carved on trees,
nothing officially recorded
of parents and children who lived beside
the dome-shaped, khaki-coloured hills
and the red-dust road that ran between Parkes and Sydney.

Walking back to the car
I notice galahs and pigeons returning,

settling back to feed in familiar territory –
unafraid of the stranger who searches
in waist-high grass
                    and breaks the silence
by talking to them as if they were human company:
even though the rows and slabs of cement
make him feel all the time
he has come to visit an old cemetery.

Manhattan Arrival

Under the wing's tilt
the New York islands appear suddenly
like encrusted emeralds
scattered over a sheet of dented grey steel –
a bounty laid out for all those weary eyes
that strain below clouds
to glimpse their journey's end.

A mass of folklore swamps
the mind ingeniously – poems, songs,
novels, myths:
Woody Guthrie, Scott Fitzgerald,
Walt Whitman, Hart Crane –

the splendour of enlightenment
that becomes a Zen moment
and disappears as quickly as it's glimpsed.

Queuing in long lines beside yellow taxis
you know instinctively
it has happened already:
                              the déjà vu
betrayal of time by a glut of culture
that floods the country you've arrived from –

your sense of expectation
robbed outright,
denied the excitement of a birth.

But the span of the Verrazano Bridge
surprisingly reiterates
the visions of heroes
and myths:
                    strung over the city's skyline

and black harbour waters
like the first thread of a spider's silver web –
awaiting the return of a master builder
who had to leave
and attend to another project among the stars.

Rock 'n' Roll Heroes

It began in 1957
with Paul Anka's 'Diana'
and the Everly Brothers singing 'Bye Bye Love' –
my introduction to the realms
of teenage angst and the rock 'n' roll revolution
that was sweeping the world:

changing hairstyles, fashions,
cars, the size of chiko rolls and hot dogs –
as the refrains of Elvis
and 'Heartbreak Hotel'
followed on the heels of Bill Haley
and 'Rock Around the Clock'.

Mostly at night and after school
I'd sit and listen for hours
to those little 45s
going around and around
like toys:
        black disc
that held answers to all the problems
unearthed in a growing youth:
pimples, acne,
'puppy love', love of appetite,
the meaning of time and tomorrow,
masturbation and wet dreams:

a multitude of ailments
that kept me awake at night
and religion was supposed to cure.
My heroes were not priests or gods
(though I prayed
to Christ on the Cross),
but teenagers not much older than myself
who were taking the world by storm:

Buddy Holly, Ricky Nelson, Fabian,
Eddie Cochran, Frankie Avalon,
Bobby Rydell, Bobby Darin, Chuck Berry,
Connie Francis, Brenda Lee
and Australia's Johnny O'Keefe –
whose shout was nothing
short of a trumpet blast
to make devils and angels sing.

But even heroes die
and grow old, write themselves off
in questionable circumstances:
get shot, overdose, have heart attacks
and spinout at breakneck speed –
as if the pace they travelled at
somehow wasn't right
and it was better to go out in a blitz:

to be remembered as being handsome
and responsible for a song
that teenagers once tossed over at night –
and the answers to what
love and tomorrow were all about
could wait until they had grown up.

Hunting Rabbits

The men would often go hunting rabbits
in the countryside around the hostel –
with guns and traps and children following
in the sunlight of afternoon paddocks:
marvelling in their native tongues
at the scent of eucalypts all around.

We never asked where the guns came from
or what was done with them later:
as each rifle's echo cracked through the hills
and a rabbit would leap as if jerked
on a wire through the air –
or, watching hands release a trap
then listening to a neck being broken.

Later, I could never bring myself
to watch the animals being skinned
and gutted –
                    excitedly
talking about the ones that escaped
and how white tails bobbed among brown tussocks.
For days afterwards
our rooms smelt of blood and fur
as the meat was cooked in pots
over a kerosene primus.

But eat I did, and asked for more,
as I learnt about the meaning of rations
and the length of queues in dining halls –
as well as the names of trees
from the surrounding hills that always seemed
to be flowering with wattles:
growing less and less frightened by gunshots
and what the smell of gunpowder meant –

quickly learning to walk and keep up with men
who strode through strange hills
as if their migration had still not come to an end.

Small School Inspection

Children offer no resistance
to a striding voice
that crosses the floor –
inhales the morning's scent of expectation
and picks up a coloured chalk,
selecting carefully
between red and blue:

momentarily ponders,
as if choosing from a menu.

The landscape of Considerations
slowly grows immense
beyond perspectives of corrugated iron,
chalkboard, teacher's desk,

embracing the outside presence
of barbed wire –
a tablelands paddock dotted
with sheep and grey trees;

while the inspector's voice
queries the purpose
of a decimal point,
Anzac Day and solar energy –
leaps forward like a fish on stones
and begins reciting
The Scholar Gypsy.

A single question
from the back row breaks
the advancing tension –
breathes in reason,
eyesight, speech:

just as the lunch-bell rings
and children file out to eat.

Teacher and inspector sit
at a sewing table
and discuss travelling allowances,
milk returns
and payment of sick leave –
touch upon
the implications of Change
that philosophies
seek to teach.

Meanwhile, the sun
grows hotter,
air in the room more dry.
Sheep have wandered up to the yard
like outcasts from the hills.
Trying to nibble
at roses through the fence
they raise their heads and bleat.

New York Address

for Tom Shapcott

Your *Seventh Avenue Poems*
haunted me all that week in New York:
those slivers of fear and joy
sharpened into monosyllables and musings –
pressing like stubby thumbtacks
against eyes and heart
in the least suspecting moments
of walking the grey streets.

When sunshine pierced
Central Park's elms, the lakes blazed
with reflections of a late summer weekend.
Even then it became difficult
to focus on the green spires
without remembering your Queensland images.

In the porno movie houses and live-act theatres
the isolates and lonely people
spoke to no one and kept
to themselves, just as you said.
Night pressed closer than stonework
for companionship
and each morning only proved
how sad it was to be travelling alone.

The week ended abruptly
on a sunless day,
left me waiting in a crowded foyer
for a $10 bus ride to the airport –
crammed among packed baggage
and German tourists
whose accents glutted the illuminated air:
clutching your little book of poems
like a permit out of the city.

At Christopher Brennan's Grave

A footprint carved into sandstone
and a line from *The Wanderer* poem –
more than adequate homage
at the base of marble
where milkweed and paspalums grow.

Turn around, ignore the traffic,
stand still and think of something to say.
The sun rolls back mists
from the green Lane Cove River
and the threat of a storm passes away.

Elegy for Douglas Stewart

The last flowers of summer bloomed in gardens
as if the threat of rain belonged
somewhere beyond a grey sky –
as if the stream of mourners
was part of the scenery and destined
to travel past suburbs and highways.

The words of a eulogy
hailed a man's spirit and the Presences
that grew out of his poems –
tributes more permanent than a season's flowers
or the colours of a passing day:

leaf, stone, bird, fish,
the landscapes of a bush or desert –
crevices of moss, streams of
cold water, blue petals adrift in the wind;
explorers stumbling to the world's end
or the finding of a child's hand in the snow.

The walls in the church reflected
a gallery of faces, names
and characters drawn from a country's heritage –
the quaint, the serious, the humorous and tragic
that fed the springs of the man's verses,
indelibly stamped on the tongues
and minds of all present,
whether priest, academic or accountant.

Eucalypts fringed the small cemetery
in the heart of the northern forest –
a circle of green spires
whose movement of colours was stilled
in the absence of breezes:

from whose crest the thoughts of friends
rose silently in the cold air –
in whose echoes the scent of eucalypts lingered
as if summer was to have no ending.

Elegy for Johnny O'Keefe

I don't know how many times
over the last twenty-five years
his songs have gone around in my head –
from the early aggressive rock numbers
to the ballads of later years:
when his voice wavered on the high notes
but still refused to give in.

Awe and curiosity stood side by side
in adolescent days
and listened to a generation
extolling his magnetism
at local dances and across the country –
the excitement and screaming frenzy
of the Stadium shows
when queues of a thousand were turned away.

A mixture of feelings
occupied more than the next decade
as I continued buying his records –
or whenever I heard him
associated with words
I never quite knew what to make of:
Breakdown. Collapse. Hospitalisation.
Drugs. Divorce . . .
In retrospect, none of that mattered
and admiration grew into respect.

It's hard to know what to think after his death
when books are being written about him
and his records re-released:
somehow it all seems appropriate
and somehow it's not.
Without my even knowing it

he helped me through the loneliness
of growing up
and I wish he'd lived longer;
but I'm grateful to Providence
or whatever it was
that got me to make the effort
of going to see him at a concert once –

and that the songs themselves
haven't stopped going around in my head
after twenty-five years
or just because he died.

'Hey, Raquel, Over Here, Baby!'

Six feet three or four
and sixteen stone at least –
towering over the crowd
at the side entrance
of the Palace Theatre on Broadway
where Raquel Welch was appearing
in *Woman of the Year*.

The crowd pressing, nudging
within itself –
swelling rapidly, yet on its toes
in case it suddenly had to flee:
straining for a glimpse of the face
about to enter
the black Cadillac limousine.

Above the excitement
and clicking of cameras, his command
thundered like a centurion's,
'Hey, Raquel, over here, baby!'
Her face turned instantly.
His face lit up, he yelled 'whoopee!'
and went dancing across the street.

A week later in Salt Lake City,
telling friends about the incident,
a Mormon lady exclaimed,
'There was a time
a black man would have been lynched
for less, let alone calling a white woman 'baby'.
How America has changed!'

And later still in San Diego,
in the Chicano parish of Christ the King,

I listened to a Dominican friar
(returning from Japan)
advocate meditation and the practice of Zen.
Around us, Jesus, Mary, St Joseph
and all the saints
were statues with black skin.
In the church's gloomy air
I saw that big black man dancing again,
joyous as a bird being released,
his 'whoopee!' bouncing off the sky
and falling like a meteor
about to explode in our midst.

The Sewerage Works

After thirty-three years
I returned to the site of the camp
where we first lived in Australia –
on the Orange Road, outside Parkes,
at the turnoff to the airport.

Remains of foundations lay in red dust
and burned in the autumn sun –
pieces of concrete, cement, tin,
overgrown by bushes and weeds
that reached to shoulder-height in places.
Under my feet the dry grass crackled.
Grasshoppers and butterflies
flew out in panic, hid deeper
in the prickly waste.

At the far end of the site
I found the old sewerage works
where a playmate had fallen in
and drowned in one of the tanks –
a Russian boy, one of hundreds
of children at the camp
brought by parents
to start a new life in Australia.

For the first time
in more than thirty years
I started talking aloud to myself
about it:
          our two years at the camp,
the accident, what the boy's parents
might have come to feel –
as if I desperately had to hear
my own explanation of it

and come to an understanding
why I'd chosen to return.
Tadpoles and mosquito larvae
swam in stagnant water:
in slime, bird-droppings
and a host of floating dead insects –
trapped by sludge-caked cement walls
that frosts and rainstorms now belonged to.
The silence of rusted machinery
stared back and said nothing.

On the way back to the car
I continued talking
as though I hoped to remember something
a long time forgotten –
though I no longer pleaded
with grasshoppers and butterflies
not to scatter at my approach

but gave them warning of my direction
and wished them well
in their new place of shelter.

Picking Mulberries

Ripened to the point of rotting
and softened by half a season
of spring rain and sun,
the glossy-black fruit falls easily
into wooden bowls and cupped hands –
while no one stands on the custom of formalities
and hastily chooses a branch
to bend low and strip the ebony burden.

Straightaway the blight's
on fingers, hands and lips that greedily
swallow the dripping sweet juice –
discarding tiny or half-formed berries,
forgetting or not mentioning
the yellow silk that could be spun
from patterns of heart-shaped leaves
with delicate and serrated jade edges.

Each cluster of fruit hangs
like a bruised and clotted offering
on the Sunday morning's overcast sky –
on the hill above the house
where we live and carry water
so that mulberry trees
might release their dark-as-red wine crop
to appease our summer hungers.

The silence of loss or anti-climax
always follows us in the wake
of our departure from the trees –
all three still coated with small chunks
of black precious stones:
pushing upwards from grey branches
that rise out of the hill's tapestry
with the misted hues of Oriental calligraphy.

Salisbury Waters

Even words are tinged with autumn
before they drift
over the brown stream's crest –
falling at Gostywick from a haze
of poplars and golden elms.

Under the bridge
a view of paddocks sloping against
each other and the breeze.
A white horse grazes alone
beneath the flight
of swallows:
                as evening
gently surrenders itself
to the murmur of insects in the peace.

On the walls
of the small red stone chapel
vines enclose each other
like arms folded
in prayer or sleep.
Behind it, over the water,
the woolshed's a pyramid
of pioneering years.

I look along the road
joining east to west,
across frames of weatherboard
and galvanized iron,
listening to water whispering non-stop
over stones and nets of weeds –
while in the distance
a man on a motorbike
is rounding up sheep

                    and a pair
of dogs keeps the stragglers in.
Only the one-lane bridge
is untouched by autumn,
                        the descent of light
and an aching silence of fallen leaves,
its arc spread like a white rainbow
over the darkening Waters –

echoing like a rattled dice
thrown desperately into the years.

Weeding

for Kate

We cannot tell
how many years it took
for weeds to grow so tall and thick –
paspalum, clover, Patterson's curse:
tiers of morning glory
slowly strangling trees and ferns.

Still, it was parcel
and part of our purchase
on a hill overlooking rows of green crests –
the old deceased estate
standing proudly like a token,
overgrown with dust
and colonies of weeds.

Sweat stains our limbs
in the sunset's light. A shiver ripples
along the downhill breeze.
We tug at knotted roots
like a pair of servants
working on hands and knees.

The child inside you
has not yet started to move –
though you laugh
and strain at the toil.
We turn up roots, white as flesh,
and our fingers touch
in the warm, black soil.

FROM *Night Swim* 1989   157

Third-born

for Anna

Blood and water stain your face
like birthmarks of inheritance
among your tiny features –
gums, tongue, nose and eyes
that cannot accept
the nursery's chrome light
without squinting.

Your wrinkled hands
resemble an old woman's,
long-fingered and slim-nailed –
twisting themselves
into the most desperate knots
because hunger tugs
through an empty belly.

Already the race
for survival is on – already
a pace being set
by clocks and timetable routines.
Your small-as-a-monkey lips
open and suck in air
like a rubberised mechanical toy.

Ten minutes old
and they wheel you past me,
away from your mother
and in the opposite direction –
leaving me in a polished corridor
trying to commit your face to memory:

dwelling on you, the third-born
of my children,
and heaven and hell's

association with the number three –
unable to forget
the dried patches of blood
on your face
like tiny maps of a new geography.

The Burning Towers

In the black granite high country
of Beechworth Cemetery
the Chinese burning towers
stand like concrete skyrockets
belonging to a colonial past
that best remembers bushrangers
and the misery of convict days –

but where, since then, someone
found time to erect a sign
and explain the fate of Chinese settlers
in the years of goldfields and riots.

While the deceased were buried
in multiple graves,
tokens and paper prayers were burnt –
small offerings of pork and wine
made to sustain the departing spirit
and firecrackers exploded
to scare devils away.

Today, as a tourist attraction,
the towers are no less commanding
in their appeal of being
regarded as exotic and strange –
guarding the mortal remains
of a two-thousand strong dynasty
that never came to rule the high country
but settled it permanently all the same
under the imperial gaze of the cold stars.

Letters from New England

They come unexpectedly like changes
in the weather, but less frequently than desired
or hoped for in moments of remembrance –
words of friendship, encouragement, hints
of a distant bond that belonged
to the travels of youth and circumstance.

Yet, when they do arrive, images
of that high country return in a splendour
unstained by the smoke of years –
when the words of old friends
revive a particular moment or hour
untouched by the awareness of mortality
or the brevity of days and seasons:

when I first saw mountains that touched the clouds
and trees rained soft mists all winter –
sunlight struck and chipped granite
or the twin rainbows that followed a sunshower.
Orchids grew out of lichens.
Moss coloured the ground where frosts
had cracked open boulders and ridges.
Herefords bellowed along barbed-wire fences and sheep ran
over green paddocks and hidden creeks.
Parrots shrieked over the darkness of the Styx
and ironbarks split like ancient pillars
struck by lightning in a storm.

It was the country of quiet cities, towns, villages,
the weatherboard farm at Jeogla where I slept
in a front room nestled between slopes
and listened to magpies singing at first light
or heard a car drumming over the cattlegrid
and wondered who was coming to visit –
where I witnessed the small school being closed down

because economics and politics
had made an uncompromising demand!

Now, the letters of friends
are saved like heirlooms –
their spelling and grammar cherished
like a precious inheritance that must be passed on:
treasured by the stranger from Europe
who felt uneasy among the farm people so often
and would stand and listen to them speaking
as though deciphering a message on the wind:

remembering the stars, the rivers, the waterfalls,
forests, gorges, hills and roads
that led to the east, to the Pacific and beyond –
wondering, if perhaps in the text of old letters
he hasn't found a Country
to which he might finally belong.

A New England Morning

Dewdrops hang from fencing wire,
between branches and a spider's web –
above vast sheets of tablelands' frost
unmarked by winds or human steps.

Fallen logs and granite boulders
wear moss and lichens of earthen grey –
as sheep and cattle stare from paddocks
like sentinels that wait for the coming day.

Homesteads nestle against a windbreak.
Tractors and ploughs stand coldly in a barn.
Rainwater tanks gleam with a dull shine
and a dog's barking runs across the yard.

Only the sky wears a crystal silence
as magpies announce a hidden sun –
and a thin trail of smoke from a chimney
explains how the day has already begun.

Jonquils

Hardly a flower to associate
with winter's chills, with frosts
and ice on windows and steps
in the morning, on handrails and pipes
that carry water into the house.
Their golden and white petals
are filled with summer's heat,
with northern suns and desert sunsets,
the wattle of Australia's bush –
or their scent, intoxicating and sweet,
full of the same arousing desire
that creates myths and dreams,
erotic pursuits and fantastic ideals
when lover pledges to lover
an eternity of undying bliss –
and the darkness absorbs the secret warmth
of their first and last unhurried kiss.

Gang-gang Cockatoos

As I walked uphill they swooped
down from the crests of trees on the ridge –
out into the open, in sparse foliage,
tearing at bark, cracking seed pods,
littering the road with debris
that dropped dryly among dead grass
and a multitude of spider webs:
their untidy red-blossom crests
and square black-patterned backs
blending in with shadows that wattles
and gum trees cast on either side of the road.

I stood in silence, trying to count
them – as they took flight, one by one,
as they dropped from branches and picked up
their flight, wings beating slowly,
calling to each other in soft creaky voices
through long shadows and out of sight –
their red heads and crests of feathery blossoms
carried along by waves of morning light.

Easter Sunday

I used to kneel and pray
with closed eyes and joined hands –
imagining the Risen Christ
in a dazzling white light of majesty:
a vision that best fitted the description
of what the Sisters of St Joseph taught at school.

It was the one day in the Church's year
towards which all the others led –
when precepts of love and doctrines
converged at a point in the Mass
and everything in my life made sense:
when faith was the last thing
that needed testing, irrespective of its strength.

There was a simplicity about
those rituals and devotions, a zeal –
the striving to perfect one's thoughts and actions
without a hint of selfishness or malice:
desiring to please God above an altar
decorated in white cloth and flowers.

Now I kneel in the same church
and close my eyes before the start of Mass:
momentarily try to envisage the passage
of decades, hear the simplicity
in a child's trusting prayers –
knowing that God has stood beside me
through illness and glimpses of death:

believing more in the mystery of the Resurrection
than in the heartbeats between each breath.

Coronary

'The land I came thro' last was dumb with night.'
– Christopher Brennan, *The Wanderer*

1 ANGIOGRAM

The screen above his head
shows him everything and nothing.
He wishes it was in colour
so that he could see
the dye being released into his arteries
more vividly – instead,
a black fluid
discharges its force
like a picture of a squid
defending itself in the depths
of an unnavigable ocean.
He remembers how
the sun burnt through
the early winter afternoon
on the drive
to the hospital
and fired the garden
with shades of evergreen gold.

The tablets he was given
were supposed
to have relaxed him.
Tensing himself
he begins to ask the doctor
questions about
his heart's condition
and where the catheter is probing.
Relax, the doctor says.
Close your eyes
and think of other things.

And all the time
the camera turns and clicks,
turns and clicks,
capturing the black dye's passage
on x-ray film.

An hour later
he breaks down and cries
when the diagnosis
is pronounced –
when he's told that an operation
is necessary within
forty-eight hours
and the damage to the arteries
is irreparable.

Only then he wishes
that the sedatives
he was given
had done their work
more effectively:

that the shadowy, pumping mass
he'd seen as his heart
really was the depths
of an unexplored ocean –
and he'd let himself fall freely
into whatever awaited him
with the sun outside
as a last image
to remember.

2 Triple Bypass

It will be months before he starts
coming to terms with what happened to him
or realising the effects it might
have on his life – on his work, family,

attitude to God or even
the seasons whose company he's grown
so fond of in recent years.

He asks doctors and nurses for
technical details – of 'vein harvests', incisions,
the effects of a heart-and-lung machine
on memory and the brain –
trying to absorb the knowledge studiously
but sometimes finding himself shutting off
and turning to face a blank wall.

The word 'triple' haunts him
with its plosive sounds, the chilling message
and impact of inescapable meaning –
as if a triple-barrelled shotgun had been pressed
to the pain in his chest and all triggers pulled at once:
leaving him alive and asking 'why?'
of family, God and the seasons.

3 INTENSIVE CARE WARD
Less than a handful of images
have remained in his memory
of the two days spent in Intensive Care –
when time virtually stopped for him
and thoughts were lost
in a sea of darkness that morphine
released into his brain.

What did I say or do, he asks
his family – when you visited or when
you were leaving? How many of you
were allowed into the ward at one time?
And remembers nothing at all
of what they tell him – like touching his hands
and remarking how white and cold
his body had become.

But a shutter lifts out of the darkness
as quickly as a heartbeat
and allows a glimpse of soft lights –
bodiless hands turning him, sponging his back,
lifting his arms and rearranging his gown.
A faceless voice asks if he has any pain
and the shutter drops before
he remembers what it was he said.

Time and time he returns
to that sea of oblivion – to those dark waters
like nothing he experienced before.
Think, he prompts himself.
Try and remember . . . See if you can't go back!

And each time his will collapses
at the point of departure
as though defeat was the only answer
to all his meditation and prayers –

as though the two days taken out of his life
were the revelation of a Landfall
beyond human description
and not to be found on any known map.

4 THE MORTUARY

Overlooked by the Intensive Care
and Coronary Care Units
it maintains an air of temple remoteness
at the edge of the hospital grounds
and a valley of forest vegetation –
the only building between
the car park and maintenance sheds
without a name or sign pointing to it.
The white panel vans that back
into its undercover parking space
are similarly inconspicuous –

except for the black-suited drivers
who wait dutifully outside
like Twentieth Century Charons.

Walking around the hospital grounds
for the first time in a week – completing
a set of 'approved exercises',
he stands between the mortuary and valley,
listening to the early morning birdcalls,
smelling grass, flowers, dirt,
touching the dew on leaves and back –
taking slow deep breaths
and hearing a voice in his head that says,
We take it all for granted.
He continues standing still, being drawn
further and further into the silence between
rustling leaves and crystal birdsongs
that fill the corridors of airspace –
trying to come to terms with moments
of fear
            and self-confrontation
that occurred while he was connected
to cardiac monitors and intravenous drips:
and the only sound that replied to his questions
was the beat of his own heart.

The morning winter sun streams
across the roofs of suburbs
and strikes the mortuary walls last of all.
His time's up. He must return
along an edge where wrens
flit weightlessly among sandstones and ferns.
In the distance, a magpie's liquid song
sounds like a sweet summons
to someone lost in the valley.
Without taking a last look at the mortuary
he turns and walks towards the sun.

5 CONVALESCENCE

He knows there'll be times when he
starts feeling depressed – sorry for himself
and guilty at what he's done to the family:
to his wife and children, his aged parents,
the friends who sent flowers
or commiserations in cards and letters.

Often he loses track of days and dates,
what people have told him five minutes ago –
asked when he will be returning to work,
the names of books he'd like them to bring.
Once, he remembers and laughs about it,
he even forgot his own name.

Going for walks in the early mornings
brings a freshness of sights, sounds and smells
as though he was encountering it all
for the first time in his life:
                                camellias, azaleas,
hawthorns, spikes of scarlet bottlebrush,
the drenching smell of wisteria trailing on fences –
silver-eyes darting in and out of japonicas
or through the glory of Chinese Lanterns hung with dew.

But the soft tom-tom thud of his mended heart
tells him all's well, that he's alive and breathing –
to walk calmly, cherish the earth he's on,
to let go of old sorrows, grievances, regrets
and accept his new life with gratitude and love:

even though he might yearn and look back
for the winged freedom of silver-eyes –
or the realm of an eternity he caught sight of
in a Chinese Lantern's golden fire.

6 AFTER MASS

After Mass he stays back by himself
in the church to pray for a while –
to gather his thoughts together
before returning to the street:
a little startled by his own willingness
to stay withdrawn from human company.

Light falls in golden parallels
through stained glass above the altar –
washes the crucified body of Christ
as though an oil was being poured over it.
The whole altar shimmers with reflections
and the sanctuary lamp burns like a red wound.

The rosary in his hands moves slowly
between forefinger and thumb;
he tries to visualise the Mystery being recalled
and finds it as hard as ever to do.
Never mind. He knows he can only try.
The Stations of the Cross around him seem awfully close.
He feels himself invaded by an unearthly wordless calm.

He kneels alone in the pew and continues
trying to pray, still grateful
to be on his own, without noise or distractions:
remembering the pain in his heart a few months ago
and how close it had brought him to death:
the faces of his children, their efforts to help –
the race to the hospital with his wife
and how he prayed under his breath.

Our Father, Hail Mary, Glory Be.
He has always loved his own childhood's prayers
learnt at home and school – with their
comforts, their acceptance of joy and grief.
(Besides, the practice of talking to God for forty years

can't die that easily, he thinks.)
Time to go. He stands up. Genuflects.
Time to leave this moment's peace,
this awareness of light that falls through stained glass –
fills the church with a redeeming glow for himself
and All Those who come to the next Mass.

7 A WALK TO BRUSH PARK

The night wind cools and blows away
daytime's prayers and troubled hours.
Trees release shadows that rise and settle
like stains over asphalt and green concrete.
Against a netball court's light
moths flutter and spin like small white flowers
spilling over the rim of a giant upturned dish.

He stops and watches a game's progress, listens,
becomes amazed by the vibrancy of
moving colours under artificial light.
Gold. Green. White. Red –
a spectrum he hardly expected to find
and wonders if the scene is not an illusion.

A joy passes through him like an electric flash
as he remembers a scene from his own childhood.
For a moment, the pain of convalescence retreats
and melts into the circle of darkness
around the park and surrounding bush.

A bell rings. Halftime. The game stops.
He turns around and walks back
slowly to the road, away from the final score –
alerted to signs of changing weather in the wind
and Where his steps will finally take him.

from The Five Lakes

'Green rushes with red shoots,
Long leaves bending to the wind –
You and I in the same boat
Plucking rushes at the Five Lakes.'
– *The Book of Songs*

1 JOHN OLSEN

i *Monkey at Aswan*
The hands resemble
a conjuror's –
long, smooth, never still.
'Now you see it
and now you don't'
leaps out and lures you
with the swiftness
of its smile.

He is humour
and curiosity itself –
angular, gracefully
embracing
with stilt-like limbs:
the sideshow barker
from North Africa
whose trademark
is the satin hat
and stuck-on moustache.

Nothing touches him
except light –
interferes with his game
or frightens his black face.
Tail erect, testicles displayed,
his style outmatches even

the boldest vanity
or conceits.

Only the gleam
within his eyes
reveals a purpose
more secret than humour –
above the Death's-head grin
that locks out
questions like a vice:

the instinct playing
a deceptive game with delicate
and subtle hands –
that finds its release
as a scream of pain
and a howl of protest
both at once.

  ii *Brett Whiteley*
The reaction by most
is a straight-out laugh: Hell!
What's he take people
and their intelligence for?
The mass of squiggles and curls
like tangled barbed wire –
or the pen raised like a dart
he aims at himself!

It resembles a seabed
with a face trapped underneath,
ignorant of vast spaces
or the puzzle of its own fate:
a caryatid whose burden
is a ledge of corals –
a jungle of weeds in darkness
where light barely reaches.

You think:
            lightning will free it –
or a volcanic upheaval
with tidal waves
to shatter perspectives and coasts:
allow it painless withdrawal
from an unbridled horse
that gallops overhead
on the beach
towards nocturnal existence.

But smile you do, and must –
one hand over your eyes
and the other holding out a mirror:
squint and refuse
to be openly confronted
by a Medusa's head

whose face is so frail
and pitifully human.

2 JOHN COBURN

i *Song of India*
My people live under a sky of flames,
an orange sun that is always rising –
my people are children of fire and stone,
their names are truly humble.

My country is a world of mountains and rivers,
green waterfields and brown deserts –
my country is a pinnacle on the earth's shore,
a stone that water has never borne.

My country is a temple broken many times,
whose spires are always reassembled –

my country is the grove of many gods,
the guesthouse of strange tongues and deep silences.

My soul is a secret open to all,
a circle for people to approach and enter –
my soul is a cup in which fire burns
and wisdom the perpetual ember.

ii *Goodbye Little Yellow Bird II*

When the little yellow bird flew away
it left gaps in the open sky –
empty black voids that swallowed up hours
and released a silence of meditation:

spaces of wonder, a temporary abyss
in which we heard our laughter drowning.

The curve and line of frail wings
became imprinted transparently on the air forever –
a rainbow of notes and movements of dance
that reminded visitors of a music-box treasure.

But sunlight also remained in the air,
a warmth and joy that winter
was never able to shroud –
                              the little bird's song
ascending over ominous shadows that fell
into our lives and attempted to create a disturbance:

invisible notes returning majestically
in long and trailing echoes
                              flowering
across the sky and upwards
in an ecstasy of yellow trembling.

3 CHARLES BLACKMAN

i *Fuseli Nightmare*
The girl laid out
like a sacrifice –
draped, unbound, asleep:
caught up in the transparent rush
of an invading night
and menacing dream –

under the fury of a stampeding horse
whose blank eyes
turn back to survey the scene:

canopy, bed, a chest of drawers,
the red décor of an eternal mystique.

A streaming black mane
betrays pace and direction,
a surge of power
that bursts into the room –
charging to an abrupt standstill
above the colourless-as-marble girl:

bursts in
        and shatters
the tranquillity of sleep
to remain poised like an upraised fist.

Breath or a cry escapes
from her lips,
eyes remain closed like petals.

An intricacy of hair fall into a heap
and surrenders itself to the floor:

the convulsions of movement
momentarily stopped
before the horse's brutal onslaught.

  ii *The Blue Alice*
A girl is falling through the air,
an abyss of blue colour
and posies of bright flowers –
light that releases jacaranda blossoms
and the cold streams of a mountain
whose water runs clear:

in sensible shoes and with eyes wide open,
falling through a cavern of air.

The girl is falling among
disembodied presences –
the watchful entry of dreams
that wait for night to come true:

rabbit's head, eye, hand, chair,
a red bird trying to look unconcerned.
One cup she balances, another falls
and its contents never touch the ground.
The girl's yellow hair
is untouched by strange light,
outstretched hands
or the flowers they hold –

tinged with fire and a shade of snow
it floats perfectly still
above the underground realm
                              from which
the blue light itself commences to flow.

4 BRETT WHITELEY

i *Joel Elenberg*

Quite by accident at Geometrics
I stumbled across the deathbed
sketch, lying stacked against the wall
with a dozen more –
some were famous, some unknown,
but all completed:
signed and framed.

Dying head turned
sideways, face sunken like plaster
along contours of bone –
withered limbs fed intravenously
by a tube that led from nowhere.
Hands that cut away
the strength of marble
were nothing more than wasted space.

A sheet was draped
across the body and exposed more
than it concealed –
genitals, thighs, abdomen:
the final touch
to a sepulchral scene.

It reminded me of drawings
done at Auschwitz –
devoid of colour, just black and white:
the stark glimpse at a reality
awaiting Jew and Gentile.

But no Star of David hung
in the room, no menorah burned
with a heavy glow –
only the signature at the bottom

affirmed
    a sense of belonging
and a last attempt at imparting love.

    ii *The Letter (To Anna)*
Three sheets of unintelligible scrawl
and an airmail envelope
without destination or name of its sender –
laid out below a velvet divan
like a Tarot pack
that has no meaning.

An outstretched nude
reclines and weeps, unashamed of displaying
pubic hair or her tears –
one hand grasping a darkened brow
whose head rises
above an unshaved armpit.

Her tears are pools
of unused colour, emptied of light
and distorted no less
than her flesh:
                a mirror of the message
etched out in the letter
with the finality of a Niobe, Andromache or Danae.

A window releases its ebony glaze
from a sky pockmarked
with stars and a crescent moon –
transparently
                falling in sheets
on the woman's letter

and a small posy
of purple forget-me-nots on the floor.

5 ROBERT DICKERSON

i *The Lady at the TAB*
Her body stands like a question mark
in front of a counter
whose glass front
openly reflects her features:

tight-lipped, pink-faced, shadowed eyes,
with hair cropped like a monkey's.

Hope silently raises itself
in her eyes, in the hand
held up before the cashier –
at the end of an interior
that disappears from view
as if witnessing a fatal accident.

A sense of the eccentric drapes
the little woman's shoulders –
as isolate in a crowded city:
whose confidence fends off
question after question
about money and how she spends it.

A warmth of colour floods
the image of her face –
skull-like, shrunken,
                        seemingly destitute:
preparing to gamble
against odds known or unknown
in a stake the future's already won.

ii *At Paddy's Markets*
The potatoes they carry in shopping bags
and the Mediterranean-dark
clothes they sombrely wear suggest
them as beggars or mourners –

gathered like a triumvirate in conspiracy
against a background
of dense green movements
that erase silence at the markets.

An Old World atmosphere sits
blankly on their shoulders –
knotting them together in conversation
under the suspicious glances they give to strangers:

resting with their loads, observing,
sharing secrets
                from past lives
and the assimilation of cultures in exiled places.

Yet an inviolate tranquillity surrounds them
and shines through their faces,
in hollow eye sockets
and fingers that resemble claws –

grasping their meagre purchases
and the companionship
they provide to each other
like water or a daily bread:

a silence and knowledge
that comes at the end of journeys
in having found contentment
from spinning, drawing and cutting thread.

This Modern Poet

Geometry, itself, cannot explain the Twentieth Century
although it can define the end beyond parallel lines
and the centre of the circle's centre –

just as it will explain the shape of the egg
and the square of the building, the snowflake,
the heart-shape of the serrated leaf

that falls in a straight line or spiral
and invents a series of commas or question marks
before its final and resolute full stop.

So, too, this modern poet – half romantic
and half a brilliant cynic, sincere (however)
who loves life as his children love him

and who attempts in all earnestness
to bridge past centuries of verse-scaffolding
as a set of parallel lines might, who

stretches out his hands for a Big Mac
and a can of Diet Coke, pauses, reflects, kicks out
at the winds of a change more youthful

than himself and wonders: where have I lived?
That I ever doubted the destiny
of the straight-falling rain or the whirlpool,

that both pierce me and drag me down
to a non-existent eternity, as I cry beyond
every Good Friday and the heart of the Twentieth Century,

out of my decades' days: no, I was not successful.
Give me ruler, compass, set square, let me construct
a poem. Let my hands and mind discover
now, otherwise, what my heart failed to understand.

Spinebill

At the least expected moments
it appears from out of the bush
and does a check of the camp:
like a small stickybeak that wants to know
what people are doing or what's said –

then, apparently assured of its safety,
it settles into a bottlebrush or grevillea
and hides inside its camouflage
to probe for nectar, quick as an eye blink –
or in the flowering red gum it shares
with the king parrots whose flock
seems to have bent the branches permanently.

In less than a week its visits become
regular –
        a surprise
and disappointment if it fails to appear:
no longer regarded as a small intrusion
that flies over heads and around shoulders –

missed, in fact, like a vanished messenger
whose arrival was vital to our safety
for the time we came to live in the bush.

Styx River (4)

Rainbow trout glide
over a bed of pebbles –
pink and brown
into grey and blue.

A waterfall throws back
the glare of the sun –
showers the banks
with a dome of spray.

Hills are swamped
by the calls of birds:
magpie, parrots,
thrush and wagtail.

The touch of frost
is already upon trees –
on grass and logs
that water has touched.

An evening breeze
whips at eyes and mouth,
stings in scratches
that thorns have left.

The peak of a mountain
hides the rising moon –
throws its geometry
against a pattern of boughs.

Sunset floods the gorge
in its tide of black and red –
throws a net in flecks of gold
across the backs of rainbow trout.

A Year at Kunghur

Sometimes it seems that centuries
have passed since I taught
at Kunghur on the Tweed –
the small school nestled like a red-capped bird
among scores of creeks
and hills of everlasting green.

A one-room building
whose only door opened up
at the foot of Mount Warning –
and permitted light
to flood in all day like streamers
over cupolas of morning glory.

Nature was our daily companion
on a road that linked
Murwillumbah and Nimbin –
running between farms and banana plantations
like a ribbon of dust mended
with patches of bitumen.

I shared my days with fourteen children
whose lives revolved
around dairy farms and mullet runs –
paddocks of jersey herds
that found their way home
along tracks of subtropical sun.

That year at Kunghur
eventually changed my life
with images that now possess memory –
an array of flowers, trees, creeks
and children's faces
which question birthright and identity.

Though I argued with farmers
about predictable weather
and the effects of isolation on the mind –
I secretly welcomed my ignorance
and chose the rainbow-bird
as a symbol for the meaning of time.

Flowering Red Gum

The soft red crowns
of each blossom
are no less mysterious
than the pale-green centres
that dry and darken
and where its heart is stored.

I searched the bush
for a colour to match it –
for those soft red hues
that were neither flame nor shell:

Christmas bush, tea-tree,
spider-flowers, fuchsia –
but nothing, nothing
matched those red crowns
that wattlebirds
feasted on each morning:

that added an indelible colour
to the sky's soft drizzle
and the grey earth
where its leaves had fallen.

Black Cockatoos

The sun was barely touching the horizon
when their cries broke in from the grey darkness:
above the boom and crash of waves
and the rushing hiss of surf.
Wheeling in mid-flight – surprised to find
a human being on the beach, they swept
down the cliff and settled in the lower foliage:
among casuarinas, the honeysuckle candles
of banksias and white blossoms of eucalypts –
whistled, broke formation, chattered,
following an instinct and feeding a hunger
as old as the cliffs and forests around them.
The sun continued to barely touch the horizon
as if its presence also did not matter.

Elegy for Roland Robinson

For two days I heard your voice in my head
and tried to find an answer
for its presence – turning to your poems
for a phrase or word that might explain
the unearthly disquiet I sensed:
a feeling that was neither numb nor cold
but removed from human desire and existence –
as if you were trying to tell me something
and all I had to do was stop and listen.

When the telephone rang and a voice
spoke long distance, I knew
the message that would follow –
trying to steady my hand and keep my mind clear
so I could take note of your memorial service:
trying not to hear the rain
or watch it run down the plate-glass window.

But it rained all weekend and beyond.
Impossible to go for solitary walks
I read your poems of the bush and its creatures –
of the Aboriginal tribes you lived with,
verses and myths you recorded, the wildlife scenes
and landscapes you moved through.

A spur-winged plover passed
over my house the night you died –
crying and circling before it disappeared
into the echoes of wind and rain,
its cry sounding so desolate and lonely.
Then I understood what you were trying
to tell me for two days before:
that when the cry of such a bird
is lodged in the heart
that moment is the start of eternity.

Deo Gratias

Let me never forget the peace I find
when I come into your presence –
when the world is left outside
the door of your house
and I can pray alone for a few minutes:
for however long it takes
to give thanks for your grace
and each moment's many blessings.

May I never forget my childhood's wonders
and the miracles of each day –
the sense of surprise gained
in praying to God for guidance
from morning until night.
Overwhelmed, silenced and humbled
by the creating power of your love.

When the world continues on its path
of hurried plans and journeys,
its desire to possess the air we breathe
and destroy all human charity –
teach me to stand still
in the heart of darkness and chaos:
to reach for the Light that entered my life
when I first spoke your Holy Name.

Stand beside me, please, as you
have always done in moments of misgivings –
when my faith is weakest, at its ebb,
and clouds darken the waters of reason.
But most of all: let me be able
to look you in the eyes when I die
and say, Thank you for the life I was given.

FROM *Time's Revenge* (2000)

Time's Revenge

Time could never go quickly enough
when he was a child
and every day seemed to last forever;
when he wished that tomorrow
would arrive quickly so he could grow up
and quickly become an adult –
even though he never thought about
what it meant to be growing up
and that after tomorrow
there was another day and another.

Now he thinks about those hot summer days
when he played chasings
with other boys and girls whose lives
he has long since lost track of –
when they followed a creek of bulrushes
through a playground of wattles;
when birds sang, wild peaches blossomed
and eternity was a meaningless word.
Forty years later he smiles to remember it
and Time's revenge hardly seems bitter at all.

Buddha, Birdbath, Hanging Plant

Three things stopped him in his stride
when he stepped out
into the garden – three things
under the great peppercorn
that he planted years ago:
the statue of a Buddha,
a birdbath and a plant in a basket
hanging from one of the peppercorn's branches.

The Buddha pointed to the earth,
to the 'here and now'.
The birdbath, filled with water,
reflected the tree above it.
The plant, a flowering hoya,
hung over the Buddha and birdbath like a crown.

His time of sorrow
vanished – as if pain and fear
had been nothing more than vapours
trailing through his imagination.
Somewhere, from out of an ancient past,
he heard a voice, 'The centre of the universe
is a bellylaugh.'
The Buddha smiled; the water
in the birdbath rippled;
the hoya stirred
in a circular motion.

He stepped back, startled –
as if someone had pushed him.
Then he saw the great tree itself.

Poetry

Getting up at night,
not knowing why –
half unsure of the hour,
wishing it were otherwise.

Drawn by instinct
to pen and paper,
the words begin to take shape –

one, two, half-spoken,
half-whispered –
responding to an urge
that won't go away.

Suddenly, for less than
a moment's breath,
everything vanished – house,
pen, paper, family.

Stars have paled.
Birds stir in leafy branches
and a wind causes
the darkness to start.

Somewhere, humans
couple in the dark.
Torrents of fire
tear through the universe.
Blizzards rage in the heart.

Death and the Maiden

after Matthias Claudius & Franz Schubert

Death speaks softly
like an old friend who visits
without giving notice –
who enters the house
without first knocking
or waiting to be asked in.

The voice that calls out
is that of a young girl
who asks Death to go away –
she pleads her youth,
calls Death 'the dear one'
and speaks against being touched.

Death continues to speak
lovingly and tells her
not to be afraid –
that Death will comfort her,
give courage
and promises she will sleep:

after all, Death is the old friend
to whom the door
was always lefty open –
trustworthy, reliable, punctual.
A violin's notes stab the air sharply.
Death speaks for the last time.

Leukaemia
for Kate

'Yes; the latest hour is, to say the least, very severe.'
– Rimbaud, *A Season in Hell*

1 Diagnosis
Now the word 'leukaemia'
will be a part of you
for as long as you live –
nine letters, four syllables,
testing your courage,
straining your nerves:

the way it takes over
everything –
shifts the focus always
back to itself.
In the end you give up on reason
and learn to accept
that you will never be the same.
It likes your body.
Already it owns your name.

2 Others Like You
Others like you
who are further advanced
in therapy
visit to offer advice –
hats, turbans, scarves.
'Besides, the bald look
is fashionable.'

So much optimism,
hope – offers
of companionship,
talk of families, children,

husbands, paintings
on a wall . . .

apparent trivia –
things that once
were taken for granted
like flowers
in the outside world.

No one mentions
the garden
of your blood and bones
where it was never imagined
anything like this
would take root, flower and grow.

3 PAIN

The silver birch
shows its black gashes
outside the window
of the room where you lie
'hooked up'
to another machine.

Another needle,
another puncture – your
skin and bones
at the mercy of a chemical cure
working in your veins,
drip by drip.

Sick all morning,
you lie with eyes closed,
face turned away from people.
When I enter
the room you whisper,
'I just think about getting better.'
Your face looks like it's on fire.

The last month of your life
has had a knife
drawn through it everyday –
razor-sharp, unflinching.
Poised out of nowhere
it never misses its mark.

Unlike the pain
of the silver birch – all this
can be easily explained.
You are passing
through the eye of a needle.
The desert waits for rain.

4 Daily Visit

Sometime between twelve
and two o'clock
the doctor arrives
to do the daily check-up.

It's then that fears
and anxieties
have to be allayed,
questions answered
and hope given
that all this is not
for nothing:

the blood tests,
transfusions, chemotherapy,
platelets, antibiotics,
mouth washes –
a host of coloured tablets
in shapes and sizes
like tiny lollies
from the corner shop.

And in some ways
they are sweeteners –
though unpalatable
and difficult
to wash down
because of mouth sores
and 'referred pain.'

Nothing, of course,
beats the best news
that the white cell count
is creeping up 'slowly'
now that chemotherapy
has been stopped.
'All good fellas'
the doctor says
and smiles her secret smile.

Her eyes give away
and she is pleased –
just as yours give you away
and reveal your happiness:

that human bit
of hope, like a small lolly,
but sweet enough
to last until the next visit.

5 BONE MARROW BIOPSY
So much depends
on so little a test –
less than fifteen minutes
in order to find out
if the chemotherapy
has done its poisonous work
successfully.

A needle punctures
a spot on your hip
that the doctor has selected.
Foetus-like, on your side,
you cannot see
the anaesthetic being administered.

The larger syringe
resembles a corkscrew
and the doctor
expertly draws out
bone marrow
that looks like blood
except that it's much thinner –
smearing it with
the hands of an artist
on to a set of prepared
glass slides:

swiftly, deftly –
one, two, three, four!
Again, without
taking her eyes off her work.
'I'll be back tonight
with the results,'
she says, running a hand
across her eyes.

The word 'results'
hangs in the air
like an empty needle –
ready to draw in your life
for the next few hours.

6 CHEMOTHERAPY
Poison that looks like water
and is meant to save your life –

try to focus on that;
not on what it is
but what it's meant to do.
Hung over you
in its see-through plastic pack
it could be mistaken
for an antibiotic.
A stranger would never know.

You speak of brilliant sunrises
whose colours flood
your room at the *San*,
the kindness of people –

letters, cards, vases of flowers,
how good it is to rest.

Presents, phone calls, good wishes –
people and words come and go.
The duty nurse responds
to a beep from the machine
and adjusts the speed of the drip.

One little drop at a time.
It all seems the same –
neither fast nor slow.

We kiss, say goodbye,
promise to return –
for a moment, stand
at the foot of your bed.

Sunrise will flood
your room in the morning
and the plastic pack
hanging above your head.

7 HIV WARD

'Life as nowhere else and a people apart.'
– Dostoevsky, *The House of the Dead*

i

Transferred from Haematology
to the HIV Ward
because you contracted 'golden staph'
and now pose a risk
to other leukaemia patients
undergoing chemotherapy –

you've adapted to your
new 'second home'
faster than anyone
thought you would:

to the smaller, familial
environment
with its goldfish tank
and Bobby Goldsmith Foundation emblem
hung like a welcome sign
to the ward.

ii

The staff are friendly
beyond duty –
helpful, co-operative,
always ready with a smile
or cheerful word:

Emma, Cathy, Dean, Paul –
night staff, day staff;
week after week.
How do they keep
their sanity

with everything they
hear and see?

    iii
The address 'E10 West'
has become
almost synonymous
with our own at Eastwood –

that small section
on the tenth floor
of RPA –
overlooking St Andrew's College,
set at the edge
of playing fields,
among acres of camphor laurels.

    iv
Medical procedures
have become
second nature to us –
inpatients and daystay patients alike:

portacath, cannula,
Ganciclovir, Intragram –
words for equipment
and chemicals
used to keep you alive:

common talk, now,
like saying sugar, salt or tea.

    v
Sitting, there, beside you,
often it's too easy
to fall asleep or say nothing –
to seem rude or indifferent:

but we've been through it all
many, many times
while waiting for your
bone marrow transplant
to graft –

for a new world
to take over your body
so the old can be defeated,
left behind.
The doctors say we must
wait, be patient.
In the end your strength
and courage will win.

vi

Looking out the window
I can see
mountains of foliage
stirring in the breeze.
I can feel their coolness on my skin.

With its blue-and-white cross
St Andrew's flag
waves below me like a sign
of surrender
from an army hidden in the hills.

8 PATIENTS

After a while you grow indifferent
to them – standing around the entrance at RPA,
under the Moreton Bay Fig trees
that partly screen Missenden Road
and enclose the drop off/pick up area:

in their dressing gowns
that sometimes don't cover pyjamas

or the hospital gowns that tie up at the back –
pushing their portable drip stands
or attached to bags of red or brown liquids
whose tubes protrude from their bodies
and the gowns don't quite conceal,

smoking or staring at peak hour traffic,
sipping Coke or reading newspapers –
never minding the scars or skin discolourations
brought down from Neurosurgery
or Immunology, from Cardio/Thoracic
or one of the other specialist wards.
Even those in wheelchairs
with or without limbs, seem to enjoy the sight
of passing motor vehicles
or just sitting among a parade of strangers' faces.

Are they thinking: which of us
doesn't want things to be
as they were before – before disease
or illness or an accident
made living not the certainty it used to be?

Sometimes I want to stop
and speak to them – to say
'No one is guaranteed tomorrow.'
But I don't. And I know I never will.

Walking away from the entrance,
especially at night –
when the ghostly orange lights
create a spectre world and you think
you can hear voices calling from outer space –
it's not hard to catch
the scent of roses from the garden beds
on either side of the entrance.

That's when it hurts the most, I think.
Them and us. The sick and the healthy.
That's when I know we're all going someplace –
up into the sky like the scent of roses:
even as petals fall
and new buds are opening here and somewhere else.

9 DAY STAY

Whether you're there
for an hour
or the whole day
it's like returning home –

to that room in Immunology
where you've spent
so much of the past year.

With its two beds
and three armchairs, TV
and hand basin
it brings to mind
images of domesticity
that somehow one's spirit needs –

the comforting
and familiar, the secure:
what's easy to touch
and understand.

Tony, the duty nurse
welcomes us
with his happy, boyish smile.
'Darling, how are you today?'
'Fine,' you reply.
'Wonderful! Now let's get you settled.'
And he does –
in what's become known
as *Kate's Bed*.

I settle down
beside you, sit and read *Talkabout*
or the *Sydney Star Observer*.
learn how hard
it is for people to be accepted,
to be themselves,
and how easily discrimination
rears its proverbial
'ugly head.'

In the meantime
they prepare you for another
bone marrow biopsy
to test the presence
or otherwise
of further leukaemic cells –
and I cringe to think
how a corkscrew needle
will shortly puncture your flesh;

and how you, too,
will have to learn to adjust
to the world outside
this friendly little room –
whether the result
is good or bad.

10 YOUR POEMS

No one saw you
reading the poems
written about you
a year ago
when you were diagnosed
with leukaemia –
and life, as we knew it,
came to an end.

When I asked
what you thought of them
your reply wasn't
unexpected, 'They're
a bit close to home.'

Impossible to imagine
what you've been through
in the past twelve months –
four full seasons
of different weather
that matches
the changing climate
of your blood:

like the time
you contracted
CMV so badly
and had to be moved
into Intensive Care –

and went from looking
like the Michelin Tyre Man
to an Auschwitz survivor
in less than a week:

that's when I gave up
saying prayers
and just lived on
whatever faith my heart
could muster
while standing at the foot
of your bed.

Worn out by chemotherapy
and radiotherapy
you were too weak

to even move your head;
but from the abyss
around each sunken eye
you'd look at me
and blink.

Now the poems
are published
and I hope the world
learns of your bravery
and applauds it
to the sky –

even though
it's hard for you
to be objective
about them
because they'll always be
'a bit close to home.'

Poetry Exam

My students write their end-of-semester exam
and some look anxiously at watches
to see how much time is left;
others gaze around the room, listen to the hum
of the airconditioner, inspect hands or fingernails
and reluctantly resume their writing.
The winter morning haze hasn't lifted.
Greyness fills the room with a spectre light.

A year ago my father was dying,
living into the last month of his life –
the man who never read a book of poetry
and, if he did, never spoke about it,
the old man of eighty-nine
who accepted life for what he'd become –
farmer, prisoner of war, manual labourer,
husband, father, gardener, lover of dogs
and Poland's greatest absent patriot,
who once cried when he told me
how much his joints were hurting.
'It's not good to grow old and live like this.'

Something holds me back from talking to my students
and forces me to hold my peace.
For convention's sake, or propriety
or whatever, I continue to say nothing
least I disturb their concentration;
but I want to say, 'Go, leave the room
and breathe outside. Listen to the sparrows
in the flower beds. Untwist
the anxious look from fingers and eyes.
Forget that poetry has to be examined.
Stand in the light, feeble as it is.
Next year's winter will be just as dark.'

Alone in Murwillumbah

'The effect you had on me was the effect you could not help having.'
– Franz Kafka, 'Letter to His Father'

Going to Mass
at the Church of the Sacred Heart,
I pray for my father
who died three weeks ago today –
so far from here, but still
in my heart: the Polish immigrant
who lies buried under
dying flowers in Rookwood's graveyard.

Revisiting the old haunts
of twenty-six years ago
where I taught in this green valley
and daily became homesick
like a lost child –
I take photos of Mt Warning,
the Tweed River
and various streets: as if to remind
myself later, in Sydney, that I was actually here.

To fill the hours
of late afternoon, I go
to the Regent and see
Farewell My Concubine –
drawn by what I remember
as being favourable reviews.

Something inside me reacts
to the violence, to scenes
of death and pain –
something I can't put my finger on
but find myself weeping for

in the dark: grateful
for the peace my father
had brought into my life.

Walking home,
the old contours
of roads and hills return –
familiar though grown smaller;
Riverview Street,
Wollumbin, Byangum Road.
Darkness blots out
the shape of Mt Warning
from which I've always got my bearings.
'It's all right, Dad,' I whisper.
'Stay with me.
I know exactly where I'm going.'

Polish Soil

The soil I sprinkled
on my father's coffin
was brought back from Poland
five years earlier –
from the graves of his parents
in Raciborów, the little village
west of Warsaw, where
he was born in 1905.

Such a fine powder fell
from my hand it felt
like windblown sand – and not
the heavy dark soil
that I scooped from under green shadows
on the other side of the world.

For five or six years the soil
existed in a sealed plastic bag
and my father never once
made reference to me
about its purpose.
Five years of living
turned black grains into grey dust.

It made little sound
on the coffin at the bottom of the grave
and the priest blessed
its journey with holy water –
as if to farewell it
to the same destination
that my father had set out for
and where his parents were waiting.

First Potatoes

Three months after my father died
the first potatoes have appeared
in his garden – small leaves sprouting
from beneath the dark soil
my son dug and prepared
just as his grandfather had been doing
for more than forty years.

All his life my father planted
potatoes – first in Poland,
then in slave labour in Germany
where he was a prisoner for five years;
finally in Australia,
in his own garden that he loved
and would show to visitors
who stood amazed
at all the hard work he put in.

Keeping the garden and living
off it, he put as much
faith into his work each year
as, perhaps, today, I put
into words:
                    knowing how proud I feel
to be writing
about my son digging
and preparing his garden for planting –
as if he was laying claim to an inheritance
promised to him at birth.

Train Traveller

My father spent nearly thirty years
travelling to and from work daily
on the trains – rarely missing
the scheduled 'red rattler'
from Regents Park station to the suburb
where he was currently working.

He taught me how to recognise
the signs of their arrival
before they came into sight –
how signals would drop at the end
of the platform, or birds fly up
from where they were feeding.

The old trains were replaced
by new models long before he died –
signals changed, modernised,
and the railway embankments
cleared of undergrowth, burnt off.
Birds no longer fed opposite the platform.

Wherever he might be travelling still
I hope my father is well, enjoying
the view that he rightly earned
and is sitting comfortably at a train window –
while I stand alone on the platform
at Regents Park and wish that I could follow.

Sayings

While she was alive
I took my mother's sayings for granted –
those lines of words that came
so easily into her head
as if she were turning on a tap:

'Go slowly and you'll go further.'
'Buy not buy, but try.'
'Having one child is like having
one eye in your head.'
Or, 'I'm not from the stepmother.'

Sometimes they made sense;
mostly they didn't – not that I bothered
to stop and ask questions,
to think about anything that ran
deeper in my heart than blood.

Now that she's dead they all make sense –
short, humorous, elliptical,
like blows to the head or heart:
spot on, up close, hard,
never missing their mark.

Birthplace

My thoughts walked ahead of me
and nothing was spoken
the whole time – almost
as if the elements had requested
that the visit be conducted
in silence: out of respect for the glory
of the European summer
that blazed down on Germany
like a branding iron.

Nothing forced me to return.
Nothing forced its presence
upon me, seen or unseen,
as I walked into the valley
that a stream ran through
and wildflowers dotted the hillside
like tiny precious stones.
Doves cooed from a nearby farm loft.

War was still being waged
when I was born here
more than forty years ago –
though nationalities knew the end
was being liberated not far away
and the migration into the future
had already begun:
the pall of smoke and ash
lifting off Europe, drifting over
the North Sea and into the sanctuary of the stars.

The room offered me its dampness,
its dank smell of timber and vegetation –
giant maps of mildew spread
across repainted walls

and a cracked ceiling
that looked down on an earthen floor:
that invited me to stand closer and discover
the exact spot where I stood in time and space.

I said nothing. Did nothing.
It was almost as if I didn't exist –
disbelieving that I had ravelled
from Australia
only to hear my heart beating so fast:

wondering if my thoughts would stop now
like parents who had left a child behind
and waited for it to catch up –
and the reasons for my abandonment
might be explained at last.

Billycart Days

He rode the red dust roads as a kid
in a billycart built from a fruitbox
along with other kids like himself
who lived on hope and laughter –
pointing their capguns at galahs and crows
that circled peppercorn trees
in a sky as blue as an exotic bird's eggshell.

Time was a neverending road that ran
between Parkes and the rest of the world:
Orange, Bathurst, Lithgow –
the beautiful Blue Mountains
he remembered crossing once
in a train that blew smoke from its funnel.
Beyond them lay Sydney and its harbour.

Barefoot, head-down, pushing along
one of his playmates from the migrant camp
he'd laugh to see the billycart
go freewheeling down a path or hill
as others tried to pile in – squealing
as the wheels wobbled and they couldn't stop
because it didn't have a brake.

Dust in the eyes, dust in the mouth,
none of it mattered to them –
just as long as they were all together
at the end of those long hot days
and there was a drink of cold cordial for them.
It didn't matter who took the billycart home
because they'd all be back for it tomorrow.

Fifty years later none of it's vanished
because the red dust roads of Parkes

run like blood in his veins:
past the remains of the migrant camp
fenced off with steel posts and barbed wire –
whose concrete foundation slabs
lie broken and bleaching in the sun:

where thistles have been poisoned
so the site resembles a wasteland,
where there's no trace of the billycart
or the lives it carried around –
but where the surrounding hills echo
with the cries of crows, galahs, children's laughter
as fragile as an exotic bird's eggshell.

The Touch
after Garry Shead

Lawrence stopped writing
when he felt the touch on his arm
and wondered what was happening.
Was it the soft paw of a kangaroo
that put its mark at the end of a sentence
or a gust of wind blowing
around the bungalow's door?

Frieda kept on looking out to sea,
leaning on the rail, below a white hat
that fitted like a halo.
Kangaroo stood behind them without moving.
The red-brick house seemed
as if it might suddenly shift and fall off
the cliff-face, crushing them all.

Lawrence wondered what stood
on the landing behind them, ignoring
Frieda and himself.
He felt the perfume of acacias and eucalypts
embrace them and heard
the chorus of kookaburras and magpies
over the crash of the surf.

Then everything became still.
The pine tree below them did not bend.
The world on the edge
of the Pacific paused for just a moment.
The rush of blood in his writing
had never been stopped like this before.
By whom and for what reason?
A moment's touch, that was all it took,
and everything went back to how it was before.
The house continued to stand safely.

Frieda leaned forward, eyes and lips smiling.
Lawrence resumed writing.
Kangaroo stood unmoved, staring ahead –
ears upright in a V-for-Victory sign.

Apostlebirds
for Geoffrey Cains

The further east we travelled
the colder it became
and the wind brought reminders of snow –

while we continued past Wollomombi Falls
and took the road to Jeogla.
Sunlight was breaking through clouds.

I remember the flock of twelve apostlebirds
feeding by the roadside
as we marvelled at the bald hills –

at granite boulders shaped like skulls and eggs
balanced in the wind of open paddocks
where sheep and Herefords grazed.

Sunday was our travelling day
and those black birds appeared
out of the wayside stubble and stones

like apparitions that ignored us
because the sun was shining on them
while winds buffeted the car.

Neither of us spoke nor looked back.
We had too much else to do
and stopping would have taken up time.

All day those twelve birds stayed
in my mind – half welcome, half a nuisance
for the unrest they left behind.

When darkness fell and snow drifted
across the ranges, their image
melted into the night – as if they'd surrendered

their place along the eastern road
and disappeared into a region of New England
where we were still to go.

The Wind in the Pines

The wind in the pines
sounds exactly the same
as it did thirty years ago –
when I stood in the same place
where I'm standing now
and looked back to where I'd come from:
along the yellow-dust road
that runs east to west
and joins the mountains of New England
to the Pacific Coast.

The wind in the pines
sweeps over the place
where the small school stood
and children played –
where the door was closed
for the last time in 1968
and blackberries began
their gradual invasion
unchecked along
perimeter and footpaths.

The wind in the pines
is always a cold wind
and the sound it carries
is the sound of the mountains
meeting the sea –
echoes like children
would discover in seashells
but no seashells were ever found
among granite boulders
or at the bottom of ravines.

The wind in the pines
sounds like no other wind
and has a touch
that makes you think daylight
has suddenly become the dark –
it blows nonstop
along the yellow-dust road
that's run for thirty years
like a scar on my heart.

Ireland

'Of such is the Land of the Immortals.'
– Patrick Kavanagh, *The Green Fool*

1 COBH

We drove to Cobh in the rain
and heard the wind
pushing against the seawall and town
as if it had something to tell us –
in spite of the icy squalls
that lashed the waves into foam.

We drove through mists
that shrouded and wreathed
the harbour – tried to glimpse
the noonday sun without success
as needles of rain wove
their bleak tapestries around us.

St Colman's Cathedral,
standing like a grey lighthouse
with its beacon missing,
pealed a solemn angelus
but could not dispel the cold that greeted
the two strangers from the Antipodes.

Statues, plaques, inscribed names,
histories of migration,
great maritime disasters –
enshrined in the cavern of a museum
as if their final destinations
were still to be determined by the mind.

Driving away was no different
from our silent arrival

with the same voices of rain
farewelling us, waving invisible hands –
and a lone seabird that hovered on trembling wings.
It sounded like a small child crying.

2 POVERTY

i

Five years after his death
I remembered
a habit of my father
from the very early years
after we arrived in Australia:

the way he brought home
old nails in a tin
from the places he worked –
nails that were bent or rusty,
had been thrown away.

With eagle-eyed accuracy,
patience and skill,
he'd straighten every one
with a hammer
on his shoe last –
then put them to good use
around the house
on things that needed fixing:

fenceposts, palings,
windowframes,
perches or nests in the chookshed
because, as he said,
'It's important
to keep them happy also
if we want fresh eggs . . . '
Steel on steel,

not too loud,
the hammer made a hollow,
steady tapping
with each nail it
straightened out.

ii
Fifty years later,
visiting Ireland and drinking
in Lisdoonvarna
at the Kincora Hotel,
I hinted at details
of the story
to Patrick, the local milkman,
who listened like a bird,
head turned
slightly to one side,
then, fixing his eyes to mine,
replied without ambiguity,
'Ah for sure,
that's a sign of real poverty.
We know all about that in Ireland . . . '

iii
That night I almost wept;
walking on the road
between Doolin
and the Cliffs of Moher –
reliving the conversation with Patrick,
wondering what the connection
between Ireland and myself
might be about:
hearing the tap-tapping sound
of steel on steel
between each gravelled step.

3 GERMAN WAR CEMETERY

The gate is heavy as lead;
its rusty hinges creak
as we respectfully enter
the cemetery at Glencree
created by a secluded cliff-face
and tiers of spring greenery.
Cut into stone, its name reads,
Deutscher Soldaten-Friedhof 1914/18 + 1939/45.

On the outskirts of Dublin
I wish I could name
the birds that sing
in these darkened trees and mosses –
below water running fresh
from the Wicklow hills.
I like to think they are the souls
of the German military
buried here – one,
two, three names to a plot
of neatly-trimmed lawns,
an enclosure of stone
where a pietà is embedded
in coloured mosaics
on its rustic walls.

Did they die on Irish soil
or were they washed up
on the Irish coast?
Perhaps both, our friend smiles,
surprised by the question.
I don't know.

The birds' singing
falls to a hush
and I try to pray
for whatever the reason –

remembering that my own birth
was on German soil
shortly before the War ended
in April, 1945.
Whatever the affinity I feel
can't be totally useless,
I say to myself.
They are the dead
and deserving of respect –
whatever their nationality,
whatever the circumstances
of each death:
hearing the words
of a woman in Carrick-on-Shannon to me
a day earlier:
In Ireland the dead come first.

We leave in silence
as we arrived;
file out through the damp air
and light grown colder
though filled with a strange,
transparent energy.
The gate clangs shut
the way I've heard and seen
gates close in films
about prison life.
A hard-steel clang. Heavy. Definite –
as if to say
there is no coming back.
The birds respond
with a plaintive chorus –
that rises and falls,
hovers like a flame
over bronze plaques and crosses –
but do not leave
their sanctuary of trees, water, mosses.

4 AT THE GRAVE OF W.B. YEATS

After so many years
of reading them
it becomes
an anti-climax
to stand in front of
those famous lines –

about life, death,
a cold eye,
the horseman commanded
to pass by!

There are no horsemen.
No visitors
except us –
not unless you count
the workmen
renovating St Columba's Church.

The grave's so close
to the footpath
pieces of gravel
could easily fly up.

Clouds pass over
Ben Bulben's
magnificent flat head –
long, rectangular,
shining
purple and green
in the spring's morning sun.

Sparrows flit in the trees
and grasses –
larks, robins,

a magpie in its glossy coat.
Lichens cover headstones.
Workmen saw timber
and hammer alongside.

Scenes carved
on the Celtic cross
opposite the grave
depict Old and New Testament:
Adam and Eve,
Cane and Abel,
Daniel in the Lion's Den,
The Presentation
In the Temple,
Christ on the Cross
and in Glory –
life, death,
art, beauty –
what more could
any poet want?

Leaving is a must
and time
will not wait –
not for workers, visitors,
birds in the grass.
Spring's colours
hurt to look at directly
in the sun
and its breeze
leaves a feeling
of disquiet in the blood.

I keep the promise
made to myself
about not looking back –

but still
put an arm around
those famous words
and briefly feel
the comfort of cold stone.

5 Swans at Kinsale

Mizen Head was our destination that morning
except for the time at Kinsale
that put the phrase 'Land's End'
out of our minds for a few splendid moments –
stopping by the shoreline, drawn
into silence, admiration, as the three bodies
came gliding into view, below the bridge,
their necks curved like question marks,
while we were marvelling at another
piece of Ireland's springtime beauty.

'Whiter than snow,' I breathed.
Blood was the colour of the beaks
that jabbed and poked under the sapphire water
flecked with silver like creased foil.
I looked for the motion of webbed feet
but saw none – although they circled each other
like enemies in a standoff before combat,
ignoring townsfolk, motor vehicles,
a dog running along the breakwater's stone edge –
then away, as suddenly as they appeared,
as if the show for tourists was over
or their morning's hunger had been satisfied.

We resumed our journey without saying
too much, as we drove towards Mizen Head
and the rest of the day – along green hills
of yellow gorse, dotted with black-faced sheep,
following the same tributary of water
the swans had paddled on earlier

and now widened as it neared the sea –
remarking what a mirror surface it had become
since its ripples carried them
out of the morning and into the rising sun.

6 DEATH MASK SCULPTURE OF JAMES JOYCE

In a corridor
between rooms of books
and paintings,
posters and memorabilia,
it looks grotesque
lying bodiless
on a table covered in green cloth,
beside a candle
that's burned out.
A white gossamer cloth
arranged over it
like a veil
is reminiscent of
a bridal bed.

Forehead, chin, nose
have been worn away
the most –
suggesting hands
that have rubbed the surface
out of respect
or maybe for good luck.

Bare floorboards,
stairway, big rooms
in a restored
Georgian House
easily carry echoes of
one's breathing
as well as noises
from the street.

So much to think
and talk about
while walking from
one floor to the next –

so much that might
sum up Ireland
and Dublin itself:

language, custom,
humour, music,
the faces of people
themselves –

and returning
once more
to the death mask
without answers or questions
however genuine, brief –
simply to stand
in the corridor's sunlight
and try to take
it all in:

the closed eyes, creased brow,
patches of
sculptured skin
that strangers' hands
are slowly
wearing thin:

at No. 35
North Great George Street –
in the heart of Dublin,
overlooking
the River Liffey.

Seeing My Parents

Both of them stand
on a corner, waiting for traffic
to clear before they cross the street,
heads bent towards each other,
speaking softly in gestures – like
unfinished sentences – only they understand.
It's always the same, no matter what the weather.

I see them everyday ahead of me
whether I want to or not –
in suburbs they never visited
and gardens not of their making,
having lived in a world changing so quickly
it hardly seems they were here before.
They never look back, never see me.

The lines on their faces
are as fresh as when I last saw them alive.
I know they're speaking of
domestic chores, what has to be cooked –
what needs doing in the garden.
Two old people looking up, peering into nowhere.
A nod of the head, and they prepare to move on.

I try to catch up, reach out
and touch them – thank them
for everything they did for me
while we lived together as a family.
As I get closer they hold onto
each other's arm, step cautiously from the curb,
out of yesterday and into tomorrow.

One Photograph

How strongly was the sun shining
that day in Germany
when the photograph
was taken – and what part
of the day was it?
Morning, midday or afternoon?

Often I've thought
how good it would be
if I'd known more
about you – age, full name,
place of birth, what
brought you into my mother's life?

Three men standing
in a straight row.
'He's the one in front.'
Those were my mother's
exact words
on the night before she died –

finally telling me
what I'd suspected
all those years she kept
that one photograph
to herself – like a secret
she didn't want found out.

Sleeves rolled up, smiling,
you stand more
confidently than the other two.
War, stormclouds, a darkness
gathers in the forest behind you.
You betrayed and left my mother.
I was not yet born.

I wonder how strongly
the sun was shining
to leave this crystal-clear
image of you – given to me
by my mother on the night
before she died.
The only photograph I have of you.

Mother and Son

I must be less
than eighteen months old –
naked, in my mother's arms,
face pressed against hers
as if danger was nearby.

We're standing
in an empty field
with a hill in the background.
Thistles and weeds
grow around us, at our feet.
The sky's a total blank.

With my arms wrapped
around her neck
she is smiling a smile of pure love.
You can see it in her eyes.
Her feet are planted
firmly on the ground.
Her floral dress hangs in folds.
There is something courageous
in the way she stands.

The setting is a Displaced Persons' camp
in northern Germany
after the end of World War II.
She has no husband
and I have no father.
Does it make a difference
to how we feel?

Fifty-two years later,
on the night before she dies,
my mother will tell me his name

and the details of our lives.
(While she spoke
I asked few questions –
was content to let her say
what she wanted to
and what she didn't . . .)

All that matters to me
is that smile of pure love;
all the money in the world
couldn't buy it
and it would never be for sale.

Today, I stare for hours
at the photograph
and wonder who took it and why,
of a mother standing
with her son in her arms,
in a Displaced Persons' camp –
in northern Germany
after there's been a World War –
in a field of weeds and thistles,
under a blank sky.

Cherry Tree

Not much taller
than myself and growing
in the middle
of a back garden in Berlin,
its glossy-red fruit
was matched in colour
only by geraniums
that grew in window-boxes
of a house over the fence.

Tempted, unable
to hold back my curiosity,
I reached out
and picked a cherry,
tasting the sour flesh
of what I later learned
to be the 'morello' variety.
Spitting out the flesh and juice
as quickly as I'd bitten,

I stepped back, speechless,
ashamed to meet the eyes
of geraniums
that watched like old people
dressed in their best clothes
and wheeled out
to enjoy the first fruits
of a Sunday morning's light
in a back garden in Berlin.

A Bag of Oranges

I

When my mother and I arrived
at Central Station
from the migrant hostel in Parkes
to begin our lives
as a family in suburbia –
my father met us
on the platform
with a bag of oranges as a gift.
It was 1951.

We travelled to Regents Park
on the south-western line
with boxes and suitcases
securely tied
with straps and ropes.
A large trunk had been brought beforehand
with my father from Parkes.
There was much talk
about life in Sydney –
and what a prosperous future
lay ahead for us.

On the way to Regents Park
the bag of oranges lay
stacked on top
of the baggage like the rest
of my parents' hopes.
I tried to imagine them
in the brown paper bag, glowing
warmly in the dark.
Were they soft and sweet, delicious?
Or were they sour and hard?

Though the oranges were eaten
and our journey
into the suburbs begun
I never understood why my father
brought them
as a welcoming gift.

2
Our home had lino on the floor
and there were newspapers
covering the windows.
During the day my mother
would take them down
so the rooms got plenty of sunlight.
Furniture consisted of
a table and chairs, a sideboard
and two mattresses – all of which
we inherited with the house.
For weeks we slept on the floor.
Light globes hung
under plain-glass shades.
My parents talked excitedly of the future.

3
Nearly forty years later,
visiting Poland,
I saw a man giving an orange
as a gift – one of many
he'd brought back
in his car from Spain.
When I asked why, he replied,
'The weather here
is too cold to grow them.
Have one. It's the fruit of the sun.'

Blood Plums

Fruit of my childhood
and a time
when language
was still strange –
when vowels and consonants
had to be learnt
in new combinations
and tomorrow was a school
that always had to be attended.

Of all the fruits
my parents grew
in the backyard garden
their colours
shone the darkest –
green, mauve, a clotting red,
among apples, peaches, mandarins.

Their flesh was soft,
almost human,
brusing easily
when squeezed
too hard or dropped.
Sweet juice dripped from lips,
ran down fingers,
on to clothes and the kitchen lino.

This was Australia,
my parents would say –
where we'll have plenty
of everything
because we work for it:

a house, nice clothes,
good food,
one day, even a car.
I never thought
what any of this meant
except when I had to learn the language.

Words came easily,
their meanings and phrases,
spelling, grammar, tenses.
I was able to describe
the fruits that grew in our garden
when I wrote compositions.

And yet, sometimes
I'd write uneasily –
remembering how hard
my parents were working
to save money
and pay off the house they dreamt
of owning as soon as possible.

The image of blood plums
figured in my head
when I wrote like this and stopped to think.
They never tasted
as sweet as when picked from the trees
and I'd hurriedly blot the ink.

Digging Time

He always knew when it was digging time
by the change of weather
and the crops we'd finished
picking that season – whose stalks
and leaves were left as compost
on rows of soil that shone wet with dew.

Come late autumn, early winter,
my father would begin to dig
the soil over once more –
bring to completion the cycle
started a year ago in the backyard
of the house we called 'our home'.

Without either parent saying much
the planting of vegetables would
soon follow – potatoes, beans, cabbages,
a diet I never questioned
but took for granted like the rest
of what was happening in our lives.

There was something military
in the way those rows took shape
and stood in straight lines –
their width measured by hand-spans
and shovel-widths as good
as any machine could have managed.

As long as we lived at 10 Mary Street
we ate well and enjoyed good health.
Now, with both parents dead
and the house long-sold,
I take a different kind of walk
among rows of freshly-turned earth
and discover the true meaning of wealth.

Marigolds

They grew lower
than any of the flowers
in our garden –
almost at ground level,

in green clumps
bordering the footpaths
and were the most modest
of decorations –

yet their bold orange fires
added a brightness
to the garden and to the lives
we brought home everyday

from the outside world
that belonged to a new country –
especially when they shone
like small lanterns in the dark.

Strawberries

Returning from school,
letting the dog off the chain –
I'd play among the rows
of vegetables in our garden,
happy to be home at last.

Whatever looked ripe
I'd sample, trying to see
if plums or mandarins
were ready for eating –
spitting out if I'd chosen
badly, the fruit too bitter
for swallowing.

But I never made a mistake
with the strawberries
that grew in a patch
behind the garage.
Shining like red stones
in the afternoon sun
they were a treasure
like no other we owned.

Their ripeness
never failed to tempt
a primary-school boy
who'd been learning
about English grammar all day,
the Ten Commandments
or Arithmetic tables
that always confounded him.

The day's problems dissolved
into nothing the longer

I sat and tasted
the sweet fruit among tendrils
and white-flowering buds –
at the same time
scooping handfuls of soil
and playing with them
in the perfectly-straight rows
my father had created
with his shovel and farmer's know-how.

The strawberries filled
my mouth, my belly and hunger –
making it look
like I was bleeding
when their juices ran down
my fingers and stained my shirt.

I never got into trouble
for raiding the garden
as often as I did
though I felt as if I'd trespassed
onto forbidden ground
more than once.
The stains on my clothes
were harder to wash out
than my hands with ingrained dirt.

Summer in the Country

Summer in the country
was brushing away
flies from your face
and wiping sweat from your eyes –

watching grasses and grains
shimmer in paddocks
or sheep and cattle
grazing beyond a windbreak of pines.

Galahs clanged over the homestead.
A windmill turned
when a breeze sprung up.
Cockatoos screeched from the pepper tree.

Only crows frightened me
with their sorrowful cries
and the way they flew slowly
like black crosses.

The old slab-spilt shed
was a treasure-trove
of harnesses, bridles, farm
machinery, forty-four-gallon drums –

its walls covered
with cobwebs that housed
unimaginable spiders
but where it was cool inside.

I didn't miss Europe
like my parents did –
nor a Christmas with snow
I'd hear them talking about.

Christmas in the country
was being given a glass of cold lemonade
and falling asleep
under a red-gum's shade.

Tomatoes

Tomatoes staked higher
than my childhood years
on either side of the backdoor steps –
below the kitchen window
overlooking the vegetable garden
and the third bedroom small as a cell.

Details that defined
home, a habitat that lives
and years belonged to –
curtains, cupboard, stove,
the hum of a refrigerator at night,
the clicking sound of a key in a lock.

Cooking, washing, sweeping,
the breath of human lives
entering and exiting the house,
accumulating over forty years –
mingling with the scent of tomatoes
that grew on either side of the back steps.

Tadpoles
for Al Zolynas

As children we'd catch them
in Duck Creek – Johnny, Roger and myself –
in the slimy green water
of clayish recesses
where bulrushes and watercress grew.

We'd cram our jars and milk bottles
with the black oval-shapes
whose tails wriggled nonstop
and heads butted against glass –
whose small mouths popped silently
as they tried to escape.

Those with legs already formed
would try to scale
the impossible smooth heights –
while their bellies
of circular tubes and veins
heaved like a bellows
containing a network
of electrical wires.

There was no real reason
for us to catch them –
to store them under back steps
or leave them out in the sun.
By next day, most would be dead –
the water smelling so bad
we'd tip it on to an ants' nest
and watch the ants eat the remains.
We knew nothing about
breaking life-cycles or offending Mother Nature.
We just called it 'having fun'.

Fifty years later,
trying to fall asleep, sometimes
I remember how a gang of small boys
caught tadpoles and lived out
the cruel parts of their lives –
how they ran afterwards through long grass
as though escaping
from the scene of a crime.

Tadpoles swim around in the darkness outside,
swarm against the window-panes –
heads butting, tails
lashing the glass –
never taking their eyes off me,
their mouths popping
just like they did five decades ago.
Not one of them ever suffocates.
The oxygen in the water never gets used up.

Roses

My mother grew roses
whose names
belonged to a different era –
Apollo, Montezuma, Mr Lincoln,
whose petals and whorls
gave off such reflections
you'd shield your eyes
in mid-summer
as you walked through
the front garden.

They grew like aristocrats
in rows and circular plots
behind bricks
and grey paling fences –
those magnificent presences
that somehow gave
our suburban lives
a different kind of meaning.

People returning home
from the factories
in the afternoon
would stop to smell them
or comment on their beauty.
'Have some,' my mother
would offer. 'I have plenty.'

She cared for her roses
with the same attention
you might give to rearing a child –
watering, feeding, pruning,
knowing what needed doing
and what time of the year
it had to be done.

My mother never studied
history or mythology,
never debated what
immortality might mean.
Her home was her castle
and she was content
to work among roses to the end –
remaining, in her own realm,
a woman who was neither
servant nor queen.

Only Child

For as long as he can remember
he was always good with words –
the little boy who stared through the window
and listened to how the wind made the grass sing.
He would wait alone in a room
for his mother to come home from work –
from a place 'out there', whatever
that meant, while the clock's hands moved
so very very slowly until the door opened
and she stood there, smiling, arms held out to him.

It was during those times of being alone
that he managed to put sounds together –
somehow welded a feeling in his blood
with the sounds it would create in his head.
Cold when he shivered and had no coat.
Warm when he snuggled under the eiderdown.
Go away when he was angry with someone.
Please stay when he was frightened
of being left alone in the room.

His childhood had become a series
of arrivals and departures, packed suitcases
left waiting at the front door
for a bus or truck to transport him
and his mother to the next Displaced Persons' camp.
'One day it will change,' his mother told him.
'One day we will settle down in a house of our own –
Have a garden, grow vegetables and flowers.
You can have your own puppy. One day
You will understand what our lives were about.'

Now his mother is dead and his adopting father.
His own life has passed the fifty-year mark.

Often he prefers the company of music and books
to the presence of other human beings.
He trusts very few people apart from his own family
and could spend all day watching the flights of birds
if time and circumstances permitted the luxury.

Words come easily, almost indifferently,
but he says nothing and sinks into his own well of silence –
in whose depths he hears the same kind of music
he heard when left alone as a child
and the wind scattered its treasure of vowels and consonants
for him to discover in the long grass.

Paris

for Brian Tamberlin

'Paris is a walking city,'
a friend told me before I went away –
a judicious man, wordly,
careful with his words;
he lived there once for six months
and obviously knew what to say.

His words rarely left my mind
but still existed in a realm
entirely of their own –
as if they possessed the power
to claim whatever I was doing
and capture that moment of time:

whether I was out walking
or just standing still –
using the maze of the metro
or hailing a taxi in the rain.
Time and time his words returned
and haunted me, reminding me of home.

History. Art. Literature –
museums, churches, gardens, palaces,
jewellery, champagne, perfume:
a list of entrances and exits so long
from one day to the next
it became impossible to take it all in.

At the end of the week
I wondered what I'd learnt
by walking around as I'd done.
Could I measure time
or predict tomorrow's rain
by the tired feelings in my bones?

Or had I discovered the meaning of place
beyond my friend's words
and the springtime leaves wet with rain –
as I visualised for a moment
every step I'd taken that week
flow along the beautiful River Seine?

Sunday Visits

1

We visited friends on Sundays after Mass
in Lidcombe, Bankstown or Doonside –
one of those western suburbs of the 1950s
where immigrants like us had settled.

We travelled by train, then on foot,
from railway barrier to squeaky front gate:
the trio walking like a model family
dressed in best clothes because it was Sunday.

Met at the front door we were treated like royalty
to a sumptuous meal prepared beforehand
with other guests who arrived for the day.

2

Children played in backyard vegetable gardens
while parents sat around dining tables
and talked of Europe and their exiles –
cursing Hitler, Stalin and how 'the war years'
had forced them to emigrate to Australia.

Clouds of blue cigarette smoke filled the house.
Vodka and beer filled glasses and stomachs
as toasts were raised to absent friends, relatives –
or the 'little ones' running around outside
in their discovery of the New World.

Oblivious to most of it we were climbing trees,
searching through neighbouring creeks
and uncleared bushland settings like pioneers –
setting dogs onto chooks and other imaginary foes
that lurked in tall grasses, behind work sheds.

Girls played with dolls, prams, teddy bears.
Boys showed off on 24-inch bikes or scooters.
If anyone hurt anybody else you had to apologise
or be prepared to suffer the consequences
from one of the adults when they came outside.

3

Going home in the chill evenings, saying goodnight
at the front gate among the scent of roses,
the sound of a piano accordion or violin music
trailed in the air with its poignant European melody.

Worn out by the end of the day we were glad
to be on our way – though we smelt of sticky
paspalum weeds and the dust from the road on our shoes.

We knew nothing about politics, the causes of war,
and our 'homelands' were now in the suburbs.
The lights of the railway station shone in the distance
like the altar candles at Mass each Sunday morning.

Washboard

My mother washed clothes
for 'the lady of the house'
in two concrete tubs in the laundry –
on the farm in Parkes
where she worked each week
and would visit from the migrant hostel
five or six miles away.

In the tub her arms disappeared
in soapsuds up to the elbows
and she sang as she rubbed
the clothes on a washboard –
such a marvelous invention
that she laughed and said it must be
a musical instrument
because of the music it made.

Her fingers made the washboard sing
with a snare-drum rhythm
through cotton, canvas and woollens.
The soapsuds burst, made
tiny popping sounds
and the happy splish-splash of water
was a song we shared – even though
the times together came with a warning.
'Don't go far away,' she'd say.
'Always play where I can see you.'

Fifty years later
the lady of the farm has died.
My mother's hands
are as wrinkled as an old grey tree
and from a distance I stand
and watch her in the laundry

beside her washing machine.
The washboard sometimes
echoes in my head with the song
of old-fashioned washing –
the same sounds that a child
once loved to hear as he played
but never stopped to ask their meaning.

Regents Park

I

Drab, ash-grey, grimy
working-class suburb
in south western Sydney –
established on the junction
of the Bankstown and Liverpool railway lines.

Named by
Mssrs Peck and Jackson in 1879
after the favourite riding spot
of the Prince Regent
in north west London,
the regal name belied
its true nature of being
nothing more than Crown Land
overgrown with paper barks and prickly scrub.

Subdivisions of land
brought schools, shops,
a post office,
the expansion of the railway line –
began to make life more manageable
and helped people to survive.

Unlike neighbouring suburbs
it never really
grew in size –
remaining an enclave
of fibro cottages, factories, warehouses
where established families
of Anglo–Celts were entrenched
in 'True Blue' lives,

where Bloody Balts
from Europe moved in
after World War II, worked,
socialised on weekends
in others' new homes,
went to Mass on Sundays
and listened to sermons that lambasted Communism
while extolling the glories
of their homelands and Europe's past.

2

Fifty years later
I drive through it
on my way to work –
remember playing under wattles
and in brown summer grasses
that grew alongside Duck Creek.

Signs on shop fronts
read in Arabic and Vietnamese.
Signals at both ends of the railway station
have been modernised
although the tracks run just as clean.
The old wooden steps
have been replaced by steel girders and a lift.
Tall apartment blocks line
both sides of Amy Street.
Buses connect the suburb to the city.

3

It doesn't take long
to pass through it – to say
a prayer for the souls
of both deceased parents
and think of the house at 10 Mary Street,
to where I've never returned
since it was sold in 1997.

We moved there in 1951.
Even before they paid off
the house in four years
my parents proudly called it 'home'.

Back Fence

It separated our yard
from the bushland,
from the creek and empty allotments
where factories would be built –
the grey paling fences
that defined where our property ended
and the horizon on the hill began.

As a child I could never
see over the fence without
stepping on to something to make myself taller –
or to haul myself over
on to the other side, skinning
knees and elbows in the process,
getting splinters
into fingers and palms.

The world that lay beyond
and waited to be explored
was more than worth the effort –
the virgin tract of paperbarks
and black wattles,
prickly scrub, white moth plants,
clumps of blackberries
where blue wrens sang and bred.
Duck Creek ran through it
with tall bulrushes that hid snakes
and blue-tongue lizards -
or the spider webs strung across grass tracks
that children's feet would flatten.

My father built a door into the fence
to make access to
the bush and creek easier –

put in hinges, handcarved
the latch and fixed everything with a washer,
nut and bolt, laughed and said,
'That door will last forever at least.'

When I sold the house
fifty years later
there were no formal goodbyes
to my old playground, no tears
or regrets at finally 'letting go.'
With my parents dead
and most of the bush sold for development
I turned the latch for the last time.
The nut, bolt and washer were turning to rust.
I peered over the fence
without having to step on anything –
surprised at how easily
the horizon could be touched.

Threading the Needle

She'd wet the thread between her lips
and hold it up to the light –
then, with hardly a pause
and like a shooter taking aim,
she easily pushed the narrowed end
into the eye no bigger than a speck.
Straight through it always went.

Even when she had to wear glasses
and old age had bent her back,
my mother's hand was steadier than mine
when it came to threading the needle.
She'd tell me to be quiet, to watch,
if I wanted to learn how the job
should be properly done.

Mostly, though, it was like
she wasn't even there –
not saying much while she sewed
or worrying about the time:
as if threading the needle
had put her into a place that existed
somewhere beyond her own mind.

The Third Face in the Photograph

Posed by the photographer
from *The Sydney Morning Herald*
for an article to appear
in 'Summer Agenda',
I stand behind my seated mother
in the front garden
of the house
that was my home
until I moved away in 1967.

'No, it's not right,'
says the photographer, a Cork man.
'You need to be holding
something . . . A book, yes.
Have you got
a book with you?'

I go and bring
the only book I have in my car –
the *Selected Poems* 1965-75
of an Irish poet.
Without knowing it,
I hold the book, front cover out.

My mother sits in clothes
she's made herself.
She has combed her hair.
Her hands are folded, palms up, as if meditating.
You can see the bent fingers.
The veins are like roots
reaching into soil.
Although she's smiling
her seventy-nine-year-old face
looks absent, withdrawn.
It's like she isn't there.

It will be the last photograph
taken of my mother
and myself – on the lawn
that my father weeded
so diligently and mowed.
The redbrick veneer façade of
10 Mary Street, Regents Park,
will be captured
in a city's newspaper –
'an opportunity' my father
would have shrugged off, dismissed
as being unimportant.

The last photograph
of a mother and son –
with a third face staring
back at the camera
from the cover of a book:

the stranger, hair windblown,
wearing a parka,
jaw set, barely smiling –
indomitable, chiselled,
almost Stone Age –
squinting into the light,
his back to a shoreline
at low tide –

himself, like mother and son,
caught forever
with two strangers
on the film of a camera
that never misses its subject
once the focus is set.

Carnations

One carnation broke off from its stem
while I was arranging the vases –
one white carnation
from a bunch of whites and reds:
colours of Poland's flag,
symbols of death and redemption.

Grass was wet with dew.
Birds sang in the face of the rising sun –
a handful of visitors was already there,
lost in their own thoughts and spaces;

in the Polish section of Rookwood Cemetery
on Mother's Day, in the year 2001 –
whose gates were crowded with flowersellers
and their buckets of chrysanthemums.

Another year. Another visit.
I placed the broken flower
at the base of my parents' headstone
and stepped back to pray
without thinking about loss or death –

remembering that carnations were
my mother's favourites
and their name means 'flower of the flesh.'

My Father's Watch

My mother bought it for him
in the last decade
of his life –
the Seiko watch
my father reacted to
almost with a child's delight,
surprised he couldn't
hear it ticking
and the size of its battery
smaller than a five-cent coin.

It never stopped amazing me
how he treasured
that gift – sometimes
holding it for a long time
as though he expected it
to come to life.
Flat, rectangular,
with a gold-plated casing and face
it resembled a postage stamp
from an exotic, faraway place.

He wore it with pride
and a quiet grace
on any occasion that required
a little dressing up –
like going to church or getting
his hair cut.
As I drove him, he'd hold
his hands crossed
at the wrists, left over right,
with the watch prominently displayed.

When he was dying
at the age of eighty-nine
it was there with him,
lying on a small
chest of drawers
beside his bed,
easily within arm's reach
as though deliberately placed –
ticking away silently,
light rising from its face.

My Father's Hammer

My father's hammer
was the old-fashioned kind,
without a claw, shaped
like a small anvil –
one end straight, blunt,
the other end shaped
like a wedge,
as if forged for something
other than hammering.

He brought it to Australia
with him from Germany where he'd spent
five years in forced labour
during World War II.
I never asked him why
it had to be transported.

For fifty years
he used that hammer – always
replacing its handle
when it wore out
with one equally short,
that was just right for him.

Fifty years heard
steel on steel ring
clearly across the backyard
as fences were built, repaired –
sheds, a garage,
innumerable jobs that needed
doing around the house.

Today it lies rusting
in one of the toolboxes

he valued so much
and I inherited after his death.
I cannot bring myself to use it,
remembering its origin
and how it'd helped
to reshape his life –
but wishing, all the same,
I'd asked him more about it:

like the time I saw him
lift it above his head
as if stabbed by a memory –
and stop, arm trembling,
like an old warrior on horseback
charging into battle.

The Streets of Regents Park

The streets of Regents Park
run in the same direction
that they did when I was a child –
when I played in them
and the suburb was a bushland
of wattles and paperbarks.

Amy Street still joins
the suburb, running from east to west.
On the Sefton side, where I lived,
Clapham Road joins Park
at the top of the pipeline bridge
and continues to Chester Hill.

Those were streets of dust and gravel
from where I got my bearings
no matter where I had to go –
school, play, swimming at Banky Baths,
picture shows at Lidcombe:
leading away but also bringing me home.

I belonged to a 'gang' of children
who played alongside Duck Creek
and its paddocks of paspalum –
in those long golden summer afternoons
that were always never-ending.
We built bonfires that burnt past midnight.

Houses, shops, factories,
an influx of new immigrants
now lays claim to the streets –
witnesses to the lives of my parents
and the generations before them
who made the suburb what it is today.

The streets of Regents Park
still run through my blood
even though I don't live there anymore –
leaving was like walking into another room
and discovering, afterwards,
there was no lock on the door.

Afternoon Rain

Rain fell lightly in the afternoon,
barely leaving the roadway wet
on the drive home –
but damp enough for kilometers
of bitumen and concrete
to be covered with patterns
like maps in an atlas that could be read
once home came into sight,

or simply be remembered
and folded away carefully
in the heart as a safety measure
for the time when a moment of fear
tries to tear the heart open and destroy
whatever it is that keeps bringing it home.

Quartet for the End of Time

after Olivier Messiaen

Piano, clarinet, violin and cello
herald the end of time
behind the walls
of a concentration camp in Silesia
during the Second World War.
Does it matter that the time is January, 1941?

The song of a bird
soars above the heads
of five thousand inmates
gathered to hear a concert.
Does it matter that the sky
might be obliterated at any moment –

that darkness will fall
permanently across the sun –
the beauty of moon and stars
become non-existent?
That debris and rubble will destroy
the remainder of their lives?

Please. Sit among them.
Breathe the cold air.
Taste the hope their tongues
have learnt to cherish.
Or, if it becomes too painful –
turn your back. Get up. Leave.

Will you ever stop hearing
the song of the bird
that weaves its way among
evergreen forests, streams, flowers –
while bombs and machines
continue to pound the earth?

A song that lingers, fades,
but somehow refuses to disappear
into the light altogether –
even though the staccato notes
of piano, cello, clarinet and violin
herald the end of time
behind the walls of Stalag 8A.

Three Boys

Three boys, teenagers,
stand behind barbed-wire
in a photograph taken on 11 April, 1945
in Buchenwald concentration camp.
The caption reads 'young survivors'.

Their legs are thin as cricket stumps;
their shoes are oversized.
Two of them have bandaged feet
and lean forward, holding
on to the wire for support.

Their clothes, striped pyjama-shorts
and badly fitting shirts
are dirty, hang loosely.

The ground is barren, stony.
Barracks line the background
where a woman stands,
further back, side-on,
beside a group of people sitting down.
All seem to be resting.

The youngest of the three,
supported by a walking cane, stares
incredulously at the camera,
as if to ask, 'Why would you
photograph us?'
He has put one foot forward
like a dance step.

The other two are smiling.
The taller of them, arms
held behind his back,
has an air of expectancy

on his face, almost joy.
It's like he knows something.

The eyes of all three are white stones
barely shining in black sockets.
The sun is at their backs.
Their shadows fall forward
at their feet, slip out from under the wire.

Inside the Holocaust Tower

We looked for signs of the outside world
as soon as we entered the Holocaust Tower,
the door closing with a softness
that belied the nature of our surroundings –
bare floor, empty walls, not even a window
to see how far we still had to travel.

A single blade of light entered
the tower through one of the corners.
How did it get there, what could be
its purpose? We wondered as we gazed up.
A steel ladder hung in another corner,
high up – far beyond anyone's reach.

We could not touch the light or ladder
yet we heard sounds of the outside world –
birds, wind blowing through trees,
voices in conversation, laughter.
Looking up it was like looking into black ink.
A voice asked, Is this a cruel joke?

People put their cheeks longingly
against the walls, closed their eyes
as if trying to remember
a sweet taste that belonged to childhood.
Yet we could not reach the light or ladder.
Nor could we leave when we tried.
The door on the inside had no handle.

Sunday Mornings

Usually, it's sacred music
that I play on Sunday mornings
over breakfast and the newspapers –
aligning myself to the memory
of going to Mass and praying to God
for a multitude of reasons when I was a boy.

These days, nearing sixty,
life's more relaxed on a Sunday morning;
there's no need to justify myself
to God by repeatedly kneeling and standing –
blessing myself, as if God needed proof
or a better understanding of who I was
by external gestures and rituals.

Whether it's bright or overcast
I welcome light on my body
as I savour every mouthful of food
by the window in the dining room.
Choral music, tenor or soprano
fills my head and heart, enters my soul
like water gently covering a landscape
and refreshing the vegetation,
whether it's Franck's *Panis Angelicus*
or Schubert's *Ave Corpus Verum* –
the chords and notes
sometimes held to the point of breaking
but long enough for me to release a prayer
of thanksgiving for the food that I'm eating
and the decades that I've lived:

this internal *Te Deum*
that nobody hears except the God
whom I'm acknowledging

by the dining room window on Sunday mornings
while birds sing and flowers bloom –
always remembering the encounter of the disciples
and the stranger on the road to Emmaus
after Jesus had risen from the dead.
I've believed that story
since I first read it as a boy.

Translated into Polish

I wonder what my parents
would say knowing
my poems and short stories
are being translated
and published in Poland –
back to the language
I grew up with
before I learned to speak
and write in English.

Though I've lived
in Australia for fifty-five years
I sometimes still feel
out of place – having
become the traveller
who doesn't want to return
after he makes a trip to Europe.

Looking at the translated works
it's impossible
not to see the irony –
knowing that Polish
is the language I'm quickly forgetting
since both parents have died,
finding myself
more and more of a stranger
to Polish nouns and verbs
every time I have
to use them correctly.

One part of me says
it's terrific
about the translated works.
Another part asks,

'Does it really matter?'
Goes on to ask more questions
about identity and fate
and why my life
ended up in Australia.

I think of my birth
at the end of World War II
and snippets of history from it
enter my head
as if they had a hidden agenda:
Dresden, Warsaw, Stalingrad,
the fall of Berlin –
the railway tracks leading
to a death camp in Poland
over whose gates
the sign read, *Arbeit Macht Frei.*

'Now there's an irony,'
the first voice says, 'Thank
your lucky stars
your parents took you on a railway journey
that lead to a ship
that sailed to Australia.
Listen to the stories
and poems translated into Polish.
You will hear
the voices of your parents.'

The Death of Virgil

The names of gods and goddesses
began to leave him, ebbing
out of his mind like water – heroes,
kings, legends he'd been familiar with –
but not even Augustus could have ordered
this approaching darkness to leave the room.
Having coughed up blood
he knew there was no escape from the meeting.

His property had been divided
among relatives and friends –
they would see that his ashes were taken to Naples,
though it was doubtful whether
the manuscript of the *Aeneid* would be burnt
as he requested. Never mind, he thought. Let it go.
His life had passed the fifty-year mark
and for that he was grateful to the gods:

grateful he'd managed to sail back from Greece
and into the harbour of Brindisi,
into the warmth of an autumn wind
that carried the blue and gold of the Mediterranean's light
across farms and fields where cattle
and horses grazed, sheep and goats were herded,
where the fruit of the earth grew from the same soil
that the *Eclogues* and *Georgics* had sprung.

It was enough to have arrived back
in this most generous of lands, as he often thought
of Italy when he travelled
across it, alone or in company, contentedly,
and the voice of a poem spoke
from an olive grove or hillside of vines,
never ceasing to surprise him, make him
stop in his stride, catch his breath –

as suddenly as this darkness, now, blotting out the light,
wider than the waters of Brindisi that had welcomed him
home.

A Sparrow's Wing

I found it under a hoop pine
in Armidale's Central Park –
the wing of a sparrow lying
like a stiff rag in autumn dust.
Opposite St Mary's Cathedral,
it became a sudden reminder of death
in the city that I first visited
more than a quarter of a century ago.
Some part of my youth flashed past
and left a shudder in my bones –
as though it'd failed to connect
with what I'd planned for tomorrow.
Then I remembered what the Bible said
about the fall of a sparrow.

Healy Pass

So we did drive over Healy Pass
as Helen Carvill, back in Sydney, said we should –
over the Caha Mountains pock-marked
with corries and grey, skull-shaped
glacial boulders, green slopes of yellow gorse
where black-faced sheep grazed, watched
indifferently, ignorant of the fear
beating in our hearts as the small car moved forward,
meeting the upland Atlantic winds head-on.
And still we were tempted to go higher,
as far as the spiraling skyline would allow,
out of Co. Cork, high above Lake Glanmore, and finally
to stop, on the platform-pinnacle of broken stones
where a wayside shrine depicts the Crucifixion
and departing souls pause, for a moment,
to regain their breath and choose, in blind faith,
which current of air to ride into eternity.

Carrickfergus

The song of a wanderer
never sounded more plaintive
than when I heard
Carrickfergus sung for the first time –
a tale of death and love
in a town where rock salt is mined.

Even the name suggested
something hard, unbreakable –
something beyond the industry
of a seaside town in Co. Antrim.
With its 'velar plosives'
and four syllables
it carried the working echo
of steel striking stone.

The song had to do with birth and death,
with days that lie between –
as the singer lay bare his story
in words 'as black as ink.'
Drawn from deep in the heart's country
it was salt being cut from the earth.

He sang of water so deep and wide
it was impossible to cross –
of the solace that wine provided
without easing the anguish of love lost;
but in the end accepted
his fate without reproach or tears –
the handsome young rover of Carrickfergus
who embraced death and found release.

Rain

Grey clouds hung over paddocks
and a breeze lifted dust off the road
as we stood and watched,
hoping rain would fall and put an end
to a year-long drought
that filled the sky with an eerie light.

Just before dawn the clouds broke open.
Someone said, 'Won't do much good, you know.'
Most people said nothing; some laughed.
One small girl in a pink nightshirt,
arms held up, ran out and danced in the rain.

For a week it rained and then some more.
Not enough to break the drought – but enough to settle dust
and allow hope to grow in the hearts of people
unaccustomed to having full water tanks.
The strange light left the sky.

They talked about it for years:
how grey clouds appeared in the drought
without being forecast and caught
everyone by surprise – and how
one small girl in a pink nightshirt
danced like a poppy in the rain.

Summer Pastoral

Blue wrens at play
in the homestead garden
among frangipanis
and trellised vines –
out of the glare
of dry paddocks
and blonde grasses
that wave like wheat.

Hardly a breeze
touches their feathers
that shine like
fragments of blue glass –
in a courtyard built
of ironstone and pebbles
brought up from the river
generations ago.

Red dust lifts
on the road from the highway,
drifts across paddocks
of cattle and sheep –
catches in the branches
of red gums and peppercorns
where long-billed corellas
and galahs perch.

Blue wrens ignore
approaching footsteps
and continue to play as if
rain will fall
from a cloudless sky.
Down at the dam
geese hiss like snakes
awoken from a winter's sleep.

In Basho's House

for Gillian Mears

In Basho's house
there are no walls,
no roof, floors
or pathway –
nothing to show

where it is,
yet you can enter
from any direction
through a door
that's always open.

You hear voices
though no one
is near you –
you'll listen without
knowing you do.

Time and time
you get up to greet
a stranger coming
towards you.
No one ever appears.

Hours and seasons
lose their names –
as do passing clouds.
Rising moon and setting sun
no longer cast shadows.

Sounds drift in
like effortless breathing –
frogsplash, birdsong,
echoes of your
own footsteps.

It all ceases
to exist in Basho's house –
the place you've entered
without knowing
you've taken a step.

Sit down. Breathe
in, breathe out.
Close your tired eyes.
Basho is sitting beside you –
a guest in his own house.

Morning Star

i.m. Michael Corry

Woken neither by sound nor light
he leaves the house
and stands outside
to look at the Morning Star –
drawn by an impulse
he doesn't understand
but responds to, step by step.

Small moths flutter around him.
Bell-shaped flowers
shine with the same dampness
that touches his skin
and awakens his senses further.
From across the yard
crickets begin to sing in chorus.

Above black clumps
of trees and slanting roofs
that white point of reference
shines like a tiny jewel
he always tried to reach out
and touch when he was a child.
As ever, it's just as far away.

He remembers the death
of a friend a year ago
and the circumstances surrounding it –
how it put his life back in touch
with a girl he'd known
forty years ago and who now lives
on the other side of the world.

Looking up at the sky
is like saying a silent prayer –

an offering of reverence
for the soul of his friend.
He thinks the Morning Star
must have shone exactly like this
forty years ago.

He goes back into the house
but doesn't check the time.
The sun's started to rise.
He lies in the half-darkness
and remembers how strident
the chorus of crickets became
while he stood and kept his vigil.

The Banksia Tree

The banksia tree's
grown straight and tall,
full of flowers and seedpods;

rainbow-lorikeets
screech and squabble for its nectar
that's blossomed like gold;

plovers guard
the lawns around it –
claiming the territory as their own.

The morning's alive
with singing birds
that live in surrounding gardens –

that turn the silence
of trees into song
from one end of the street to the other.

A lone magpie
ignores them all –
releases its song of liquid vowels,

while the sun
climbs over a parapet of foliage
that crowns the banksia
growing straight and tall.

In the Boardroom

for Tony Garnett

'Certificates of Appreciation'
line one side
of the grey room.
At the other end, paintings
bought at an exhibition,
done by children
with Down's syndrome.

Hard to equate
it all somehow – benevolence,
corporate sponsorship,
a maze of corridors
and cubicles
where employees sit
at computers
and help the 'wheels
of industry' grind on.

Across the corridor,
barely seen through
open slats,
the sun peers in
and warms the eye –
scattering a bottlebrush's hues
the colour of pink shells.

Waiting for a friend,
drinking tea
and trying to read –
the living, human element
of the surroundings
remains constant, persistent.

Of the paintings,
'Happy Feelings' by Rebecca Dixon
could be mistaken
for a Paul Klee.
Another, by Alison Hall,
shows a blue bird
standing on
the branch of a tree.
Trapped behind glass, its song
is silent and real.

The Deep End of the Pond

Curious to see how deep
was the pond
I plunged my hand
into the deepest end –
but quickly withdrew
when I felt the cold
encircle my arm like an icy clamp.

Trying again, more cautious,
I anticipated
the grasp of darkness and cold –
as my fingers probed
the depths for stones and slime
and my arm descended lower and lower.

Nothing. Nothing to feel
and discover.
The pond was deeper
at its lowest end
than I'd ever imagined
while standing at its edge
in daylight or in darkness.

Edging away from
the untouchable bottom –
towards lily pads and duckweed
at the other end,
my fingers encountered
stones, mud, tubular stems
snaking to the pond's perimeter.

An inexpressible joy
passed through me
as flesh made contact

with fibrous matter –
feeling an affinity
with what I understood
and not what had evaded me.

I stood up, stepped back
and took measure
of what I'd just done –
seeing a fish surface
from the deepest end
and turn on its side
like a knife waiting in the water.

Going Fishing with My Son

for Andrew

First time out for me
beyond the Heads – sighting dolphins,
a submarine, tankers edging
towards an unreachable horizon,
not quite sure how the day
will end – but already
pleased to have taken the first steps
in going fishing with my son.

He points out schools
of Australian salmon – how seagulls
swoop and hover above the water,
their flight patterns
revealing the location and speed
at which the fish travel.
Time and time we miss a catch,
travel out and back in a circle.

Cockatoos screech from
cliffs ahead of us – gleaming
like snow beyond Blue Fish Point.
Gannets dive. Cormorants swoop.
A flock of seagulls rides
the waves around us like royalty,
ignoring the human element
bobbing like flotsam on a sea of jade.

The glare of light's so bright
it sometimes blinds
and creates illusions of distance –
between where I'm sitting
and where the boat's heading for.
I mention it and my son
points to the anchor. 'Don't worry, Dad.
We're not going to crash. We're safe.'

At the end of the afternoon
I'm sunburnt but happy,
remembering the struggle
of kingfish and trevally as I pulled
them up from glassy black depths –
the photos we took to record
the day's slow passage
that left me tired but not exhausted,

remembering the way my son
showed me how to cast a line
and its gradual drag through depths
less opaque than human kinship –
or explaining the need to wait patiently
for the bait to lure its prey –
how surface reflections often hide
what's lying in front of us all the time.

Swimming in Jervis Bay

So far from Europe
but not from the sea
that rushes in like a wide river
between Bowen Island
and Point Perpendicular –
just as it's done for centuries
beyond my counting and imagination.

Memories of my birthplace
come to mind
as I dive into the cold water –
especially the echo of a word
that describes that part of Germany
where I was born
in a green-and-yellow timber room
in the province of Westphalia.
The guidebooks call one part of it *Sauerland*,
meaning 'difficult' and 'hard' –
an area of mountains, forests, lakes, rivers:

its people survivors and victors
against the elements, wars
and each other's collective destinies.

I change from stroke
to stroke – dare not go further
than my ability allows.
The wind increases its strength.
The rising tide pushes me towards the shore.
Waves crash with a vehemence.

Staggering on to the sand –
even as I dry off and take a last look at the sea –
the water's iciness and the word

'Sauerland' remain trapped
in my head like fish.

Nothing's changed. Landmarks
in the distance – water, sweep of wind,
pelicans sailing like kites
pulled along by invisible strings.
I remember a painting by Chagall
called *Time is a River without Banks*.

Falling Asleep on the Sand

Like sinking into
the ocean itself –
down into a green trough
that gets darker and darker

until you no longer hear
the crash of surf
or waves that pounded you
while you swam.

Down you go,
past the burning sun –
deeper into the darkness
that patiently waits for you,

past floating weeds
and the shoreline's rocks
where children play
and colourful snorkels bob.

There is no clock
to measure the time you're away
in the place where
minutes and seconds don't exist –

no compass to point
in the direction you're going
and no sign to show
where you've actually arrived.

When you wake
you've travelled further
than the water at your back
could have taken you –

water, sea, ocean,
call it whatever you like.
Best of all, fingers trailing sand,
you return with strange tales to tell.

Hyams Beach

Black cockatoos
in the banksias
and dolphins in the bay –
two images
belonging to Hyams Beach
at the end of a summer's day:

that scimitar-shaped curve
of white sand
enclosed by coastal heath,
dunes of marram grass
and pigface
like a protective hand.

A man is walking his dog.
Sand castles wait
for high tide.
Ribbons of sea grass
and bundles of kelp
lie scattered like rags.

Holiday crowds
have gone home –
the Australia Day
long weekend is over
and Hyams Beach becomes
a different place:

where dolphins swim
like pets along the shore
and black cockatoos
allow you to pass
without voicing
their harsh cries –

where a lone seagull
stalls like a flag in the air
before choosing
its direction of flight.
The tide rises. Waves crash.
Hyams Beach belongs to the night.

The Presence I

after Garry Shead

There it was again – there,
a kangaroo's head and shoulders growing
out of the side of a hill! Kangaroo?
Or light moving over stones
and grass, playing a trick on eyes,
reshaping earth to resemble an animal
on a hill eroded by sea winds?

Lawrence sat
with his back to the shape
that peered at him as if trying to read
over his shoulder – head cocked
to one side, quizzingly, its ears
like giant antennae pointing to the sea.
He would ignore it, pretend it did not exist.

Freida lay stretched out
like a mermaid against the veranda's
railing, cigarette in hand –
a model posing against sea and sky
or resting in the arms of a breeze.
Neither Freida nor Lawrence mentioned the animal.

Yet, there it was again,
not separated from the land and moving
but part of the yellow hillside –
almost tilting, sliding off,
growing out of it like a strange stump!
Why were they suddenly within arm's reach of it
when neither of them had made a move?

New England Farmer

Often he would catch me
by surprise – the way he'd appear
in the distance and casually
walk across the paddocks,
his dog beside him or at his heels –
after I'd arrive at work,
and say, 'G'day, how's it going?'

His property bordered
the school where I taught
on the Tablelands, the high country
that lay among granite boulders
and treetops that clouds caught on
as they rolled in from the Pacific coast
and brought the rain,
the drizzles and mists – and when they did
we'd go indoors, to the fire,
talk about the city and the bush
before the hours of classes started.

Or, standing outside,
the sun warming our faces,
I'd watch him peer into the fenced-off
distances, drawing on a cigarette
that was never absent from his lips –
as though he could see through
the forest and hills, out to where
Herefords grazed and a brown dam
mirrored the moving sky,

as though he was listening to a song
beyond those that magpies
and parrots released
from the green windbreak of pines

that grew in the schoolyard –
or, he'd point out the weakest lambs
that straggled behind their mothers,
how crows watched patiently
from barbed-wire fences.

It was his silences, though,
that intrigued me the most
in those morning conversations –
the long, almost-shy pauses
between breathing and actual sound.
It was then I'd hear
the forest and paddocks
speaking in a wind-carried tongue
I'd never heard before or since –
and I began to learn of a country
that existed beyond the city and the bush.

To Kenneth Slessor

After writing all those poems
about Sydney Harbour and the sea, exotic places
and travellers with foreign names,
your mortal remains ended up
in Rookwood Cemetery, under a pink rosebush,
beside Noela, your first wife,
as you requested in your will –
in the Sunken Garden, surrounded
by sandstone memorial walls.

The only water's in the central pond
where golden carp lie indolently
under broad waterlily pads.
Blackbirds and willy-wagtails
contend for airspace with their songs
in pine trees and oleanders.
Time, too, seems caught between
the desire to escape or come in from the heat –
not that there's much room to move
in that shaded, narrow corner,
in what's left of the late afternoon summer hours
as a cortege arrives at the crematorium
and workmen are cementing another row
of nice walls, all within earshot of each other.

I never took your advice at a party
and anglicised my name
as your family did theirs
when Schloessor became Slessor
and so much easier to pronounce and spell.
What should I have changed Skrzynecki to –
Smith? Sullivan? Short? Sheehan?
I always liked the letter S.
Would it have made 'things easier'

as you said but never explained.
Somebody else came up to speak to you
and the conversation was never finished.

The air's heavy with the scent
of spring's last flowers and summer's
first intoxicating crops –
roses, gardenias, port-wine magnolias
arranged around small pebbled pathways
that are currently undergoing 'reconstruction'.
A jacaranda leans over the wall
and drops its blue-bell flowers
among pine bark, leaves and dry petals.

Seats and terracotta figurines have been added
since your ashes were interred.
One, of an Italian peasant girl with an empty basket,
nearest to you – head turned away,
with a fierce, indignant look – might have
pleased you the most, I think.

Over the Eastern Road is the Islamic Burial Ground,
closer by is the Chinese Section.
One would think that the world
today has chosen to bury its dead
behind the steel gates of Rookwood Cemetery.
I wonder if you had any idea
that the Sydney you loved so much
was going to become a global village?

Time's up and I have to go
but I know it won't be long before I'm back,
that I'll drive past like I've done
so many times in the last thirty years –
only now my thoughts will be with you
behind the sandstone wall and garden of roses.
My parents are buried in the Polish Section

and one day I'll be there too.
It's not far away, less than ten minutes
at a leisurely pace, out of the heat,
under the eucalypts and wattle trees –
quite close, really. No water to cross,
no ferries, yachts, trams or buses
and time is something that won't exist.
Maybe our spirits can meet along the road
and have that conversation we never finished.

Jeogla (2)

Enough to see
how the rising sun
melted the morning frost –
or to count the geese
walking across the front garden
and up to the top paddock.

Enough to know
that summer and winter
were friends I could trust –
who welcomed me
into their New England clan
like a relative recently-discovered;

or to stand in the creek
out of whose heart
a rainbow rose one afternoon –
drenching me in a golden mist
I reached out to touch
but couldn't hold.

Enough to be startled
by a flock of crimson rosellas
bursting out of a stringybark forest –
or to fall asleep
in a weatherboard house
surrounded by hills and granite chasms.

Time was the measure
of a strange interlude
in what came to be known
as 'living away from home' –
teaching at a one-teacher school
and having to learn a new set of rules:

that you never argued
with the seasons, with farmers
or the old-fashioned ways –
where a smooth piece of quartz
souvenired from the Styx River
became a reminder of mortal days.

The Year the Drought Ended

It was the year the drought ended
at Jeogla and I arrived
to take up my first teaching appointment
in a small school,
high in the New England ranges –
an eight hours' drive from home.

In winter the weather was colder
than I'd ever known – full of
black frosts and minus degree temperatures;
ice on the pipes and water tanks
made water in the mornings
impossible to run.
Indoor fires warmed everyone
and those places in the heart
where loneliness and dark thoughts
welled to spilling over.

In summer the views were
more than breathtaking –
stunning me into silence and awe,
unable to find words to describe
the flight of eagles, waterfalls and gorges,
the ascent of temperate forests
up a mountainside,
the tips of trees catching on clouds.

It was the year I began
to publish poetry in journals
other than student publications –
where the need to communicate
with the outside world was greater
than the need to eat
or look after bodily comforts.

People, places, animals, birds,
the fourteen faces
of children I was being paid
to teach – to prepare them for life
on the New England ranges
or the towns and cities beyond.

Hard to say, now, whether
I succeeded or failed – what influence
my life had made on theirs
or theirs on mine:
all of us caught in the daily whirlpool
of minutes and hours, weather that changed
from blazing sun to pouring rain
in less than an hour.

It was the year I grew up
like never before –
learnt independence and self-reliance
without asking for those
lessons to come into my life;
read poetry as if my life depended on it
as well as the lives of poets.

My past life was a house
I'd brought along with me
but in the process its doors had become
unhinged, its windows cracked,
furniture knocked about
and there was much that had to be mended.
It was 1967 and I'd arrrived at Jeogla.
It was the year the drought ended.

Waiting at the Airport

for Karen Stapleton

Dubbo's sun rises slowly
and brightens the distant hills –
turns the mist hanging over paddocks
into colours of blue smoke.

Voices merge quietly in Departures.
The TV monitor brings news
from Australia and around the world.
Terrorism, petrol prices
and interest rates dominate
the visual seconds.

The winter morning is not
as cold as predicted.
The 'wind sock' at the edge
of the tarmac is blowing to the east
and the Union Jack is flapping.
The airport buildings
are suffused with the same
soft light that changes
from gold to a caramel-brown.

The drone of engines grows
closer, louder – as the plane
from Sydney lands.
Day in, day out, this happens in Dubbo
and in regions over New South Wales –

where paddocks lie in the morning sun
and the damp brown earth
absorbs its rays – where
crops ripen, animals graze
and satellite dishes carry news of the world
across rivers and mountain ranges.

In half an hour or less
I'll be gone, flying into the face
of the sun, over patchwork colours
that belong to farmers and the seasons –
wondering what might be happening in Sydney
or somewhere else in the world,
poignantly remembering yesterday in Dubbo.

Six Poems for PC

1 FIRST LOVE

Uncertain of himself, nervous,
lost for words – he finds the edge
that existed between them
forty years ago
is still there, sharp as before.
What to say, and how to say it,
becomes a challenge
he dares and dares not take up.

How far should he reach out
for the hand that's there,
that waits for him in a crowd
of moving, mourning faces –
that counters its grief
with eyes that haven't changed
and dissolve his approaching reluctance
into the afternoon heat surrounding them.

The dance in a school hall
flashes to mind – music
from the *Barn Dance* and the *Pride of Erin*;
the bashful touch of hands;
meeting at a bus stop
next to the railway station – watching her
walk away in a green and white uniform
in the direction of where she lives.

Four decades of tomorrows
never materialised
in his dreams – their ghosts left
like ashes from a burning house.
The memory of first love hits him hard
in the heart – and he smiles

as he finally steps over the edge
indifferent to where he may or may not fall.

   2 EYES
The trees on the corner
of Albert and Dickson
would watch us
and say nothing –
the two students
at the end of a school day
hurrying to meet
for however long they could
because a train
or bus had to be caught.

The trees watched
and said nothing
nor the roadway
and houses.
Birds in the branches
continued singing, no doubt.
Which of us
was the first to speak
in that uncomfortable silence
on those hot afternoons?

The trees on the corner
were like best friends
watching in case
we were caught by teachers
or parents – as we
stumbled over words and futures
we had no idea existed.
Who could have foreseen the illness
that would take you
through the Gates of Hell and back?

Laughing, holding hands,
we said everything and nothing
as best we could.
Today, we meet and agree
how everything's changed
except our eyes –
and what they saw
on the corner of Albert and Dickson
forty years ago
they still see today.

3 Joy

We sleep on different sides
of the world
and memories bind
the lives we've become
since we said goodbye
to our teenage years.

You live far
beyond those suburban corners
where we'd meet
after school – always hurrying,
anticipating what?
I expected nothing
beyond the moment of seeing you
and remember only joy.

For me, light shone
at the 414 bus stop
even when the sky was grey.
Why deny that?
Time flew around us
like a swallow and left
a beautiful curve
in the air for us to follow;
but we didn't.

The colours of the 414 bus
were the same
yellow and green that I saw
years later, in a painting called
'Cornfield With Crows'
by Vincent van Gogh.

If we'd only known
then what we know today –
that crows over a cornfield
mean nothing to teenagers living
in a moment of joy.

4 REASONS

There will always be reasons
for your return
and if none exist
you will search until
you find one.
The need is in your blood.

Before you were conceived
a seed was sown
in your blood by the wind;
now it has grown and its branches
reach into the sky.
You have to follow them
whether you want to or not.

You create new memories
as you travel
but old ones follow you
like the scent of a perfume
carried by the wind.
A man uncertain
of his heritage tastes the wind
and becomes haunted by it.

He cannot explain the reason
but his search
becomes his reason for living.

Unlike the man
you will always be able
to find reasons
and explain them.
That is your secret strength.
You are a handful of air.
You are also
as indomitable as falling water
that finds its own level
and returns to its source.

5 TERN

i

Over dinner
you talked about
life in America
and I remember
you saying
how you disliked
driving at night
in the snow;

but a different kind
of journey
into darkness began
when your brother Michael's death
brought you
to Australia last year –
different from anything
you'd ever travelled to before.

Don't ask me
to describe it with geography
or direct conversation.
There are no guideposts
to where it begins or ends.
You have to set out and arrive alone.

    ii
Last week
I watched a lone tern
flying headlong
into a wind tearing
across Jervis Bay –
a wind that lashed
the bay and beach,
whipping salt and sand
into eyes and mouth.

Many times
the tern hung motionless –
seemingly doing nothing –
about to fall
or be carried away.
Small, vulnerable,
like a paper kite, it rode
the currents of air
as it journeyed above the spray
from the white-caps
and water so dark blue it looked black.
I wish you'd been there to watch it.

6 CONVERSATIONS
He speaks to her
more often
than he will admit –
to the girl
who validated his existence

as a teenager
long before he ever thought
about the meaning
of the word.

Pure joy
when he remembers
the words of 'Puppy Love' –
even though
he felt invisible
every time he said goodbye
to her at the railway station
after school.

Standing before her
he became a shape
without a shadow –
a leaf that fell into a river
and was immediately swallowed up.

Waiting to meet her
was all those
contradictions and more.
Had the moon
told him he was crazy
he would have said he didn't care.

Now the conversations
are more discreet
and carried out in his heart.
Far, far away from her
they've become
echoes of freedom and loss.

Meanwhile, his soul
has become invisible –
as if to confirm
what was always intended for it –

a breath
that follows the wind – no matter
what direction
the wind is blowing.

Seabirds

Seabirds resting on the rockshelf –
seagull, gannet, tern,
the sooty oystercatcher with scarlet bill.
Walking towards them
none flies away, none feels threatened –
as if we understood each other
and the reason for being there.

Jervis Bay shines blue with reflections,
its winds ruffle their feathers
and throw salt in my face –
its horizon stretches like a trip wire.
Standing among the seabirds
where the rockshelf becomes water
the wind blows through me as if I didn't exist.

Turning Sixty

The sun rose like the morning before.
I drank my cup of tea
and took the dog for a walk.
Along the creek that runs
through the reserve
frogs croaked, birds sang,
balsams and nasturtiums
shone with autumn light.

Telephone calls and cards
from family and friends
brought congratulations, best wishes
for happiness and good health.
I thought about my parents
and wished they were still alive
so we could talk about
our early days in Australia.

Lunch with my wife
in North Sydney, at a restaurant
beside Luna Park's laughing face –
while ferries and harbour cruisers
travelled past with people
enjoying the weather and Sydney's sights.
Soldiers dropped on ropes from the Harbour Bridge
and emerged like heroes from the water.

Dinner at my eldest daughter's home
with the whole family
brought the day almost to an end –
with a cake being cut, candles
blown out and 'Happy Birthday' being sung.
I remembered the morning's walk along the creek –
the birdsongs, frogs, midges in the rising light,
how the whole reserve clamoured with life.

Poems from Victoria
for Kate

1 FROM QUEENSCLIFF TO SORRENTO
There was something mythic
about the way the ferry moved
from Queenscliff to Sorrento
on the other side of Port Phillip Bay –
its white hull gleaming in the morning sun
like the sides of a giant caravel.

Eyes shaded, we stood on the headland
and pointed out landmarks
we knew little or nothing about.
The water shone like diamonds
and revealed the kind of treasure
that didn't need speaking about.
For a moment we ceased being tourists
and passed into history ourselves.

2 AT TEDDY'S LOOKOUT
We parked the car
and took the shorter walk
down to Teddy's Lookout –
a timber platform overlooking
the Great Ocean Road at Lorne
we'd discovered after
leaving home five days earlier.
Behind us – beyond the platform
and currawongs in the treetops –
the ocean sparkled in misty light
and a rainbow was forming.
We asked a local, walking her dog,
to take our photo. She
remarked about the rainbow.
'Like it's appeared on cue.'
I said nothing. Home seemed

to be on the other side
of the world – and I remembered
how far we still had to travel.

3 GRAMPIANS DETOUR

i
Before reaching Ararat
we detoured via the Grampians
to see close-up the damage
done by recent fires
and how the trees were growing back.
The locals said, 'It's not to be missed.'

Leaving the main road at Dunkeld
we kept looking at Mt Sturgeon
and Abrupt – as though
we needed their guidance
through the blackened stone country
and were worried about getting lost.

Farmhouses. Dirt turnoffs. RMBs.
Motor vehicles speeding
in the opposite direction.
The temperature had dropped.
Sheep. Cattle. Smoke rose
from logs burning in paddocks.

ii
The Grampians were a detour
yet they challenged us
to stop at Mirranatwa Gap –
to walk to its edge and peer
into a ravine that could have been
an entrance into Middle Earth.

Green colours of every shade
struggled through earth and ash.

Ogre-shaped boulders reared up,
stared back defiantly, skull to chest.
Dead trees lay fallen
like warriors in battle.

Cold air sliced into our lungs –
caught us off guard
with what we thought and spoke.
We stood silenced, numbed –
as if we'd recognised something
of ourselves in the landscape.
Ararat still lay on the map.

4 CROSSING THE BORDER

We were surprised
how little time it took
to cross the border
between Echuca and Moama –

from the motor inn
we were staying at
to Horseshoe Lagoon
on the other side of the Murray.

Leaving the car
we walked to the bridge
built over the lagoon.
Ducks swam below us
and cockatoos screeched

in the grey river gums
whose tangled roots lay exposed
like giant nerves
along the eroded banks.

Leaves fell in spirals.
A breeze brushed our faces
imperceptibly, almost in a caress.

The seconds ticked away
as if they were trying
to tell us something
about time and distances –

about people travelling together
and what pauses on a journey
like this can come to mean.

Returning from the bridge
to the car and back
to the main road took longer
than it did to arrive –

as if we'd gained
some kind of knowledge
about ourselves
from standing on the bridge
and didn't want to leave
the Murray behind.

Immigration Bridge

commissioned for the Immigration Bridge Project,
Lake Burley Griffin, Canberra

Built by men and women
across Lake Burley Griffin
long before concrete
was poured or a single bolt
driven through stainless steel –
and cables strung like tightropes
across air and water.

Whether they came as convicts,
exiles or free settlers
they brought their names
from every part of the world –
their dreams and hopes, fears,
the lives of their unborn children –
with their Old World possessions packed
into wooden trunks and suitcases.

Shades of green and gold
welcomed them like relatives
without saying a word.
They breathed the scent of eucalypts
and heard a bird's laughing song.
Leaning over a ship's rails
they waved to strangers below them.

Standing at the foot of a bridge
they were building
on the shores of Lake Burley Griffin
they remembered families,
homelands, names that rang
as moments of discovery or loss –
all standing like explorers
beneath the Southern Cross.

Under the Brandenburg Gate

I stood beneath the Brandenburg Gate
and looked back down
the avenue of linden trees
I'd just walked along – at the crowd
moving in all directions, each face
going somewhere, yet seemingly nowhere at all.

I felt the heat of a summer's sun
and the glare of an open sky –
the longer I stood and got my bearings
to find out where I'd come from.
For a moment, I seemed to be lost.

I looked up at the Quadriga,
classic symbol of beauty and peace –
at the four horses straining
and stamping in a forward direction
yet standing stock-still,
immovable as the Brandenburg Gate –

and the face of the winged figure
who drove them – stern, indomitable –
yet somehow vulnerable, lost,
full of human indecision like the faces
of those who passed underneath.

I remembered this was the country
I'd been born in – further to
the northwest, where the Rhine flowed
and castles stood proudly
under the same sun, stock-still,
as the Quadriga and Brandenburg Gate.

Suddenly I realised I wasn't lost
and knew exactly why I was in Berlin –
though I was participating
in a poetry festival under the auspices
of governments and private enterprise.

I stepped out from under the Brandenburg Gate
and felt the sun on my face
like the blast from a furnace, drawing me back
towards the avenue of linden trees –
lost among the thousands of faces
going nowhere and somewhere
in that beautiful moment of grace.

Home from Berlin

Home from Berlin
it takes a week
for the jet lag to leave my body –
for my senses to readjust
to the southern hemisphere
where 'home and hearth' belong.

Unexpected moments
bring images of Berlin to mind
with postcard clarity –
a kind of delayed recognition
not experienced
while I was there.

How else to explain
that I can still smell the trees
when I walked along
Unter den Linden –
or the sound of conversations
among shoppers crossing *Alexanderplatz* –
the slow grind of tram wheels
outside the Jewish synagogue
written into history on 9/11/1938
in what's become known as *Kristallnacht*?

Over and over
they return – smells,
tastes, touches,
souvenirs that can't be wrapped
in paper for the long trip
back to Australia:

reminders
of the country

I was born in
more than fifty years ago
before emigrating to Australia
with my parents.

And why Australia –
why not Canada or South America –
anywhere that a semblance
or affinity of heritage
might be found and laid claim to?

With the jet lag disappearing,
memories of warm nights
return, long hours
of daylight, poetry readings,
the inescapable scent of linden trees
sweeter than before –
a realisation that somehow, mysteriously,
I've brought 'home and hearth'
back to Australia with me.

Family Portrait
for Anna

All my life I've lived
with the photograph
my mother took with her
when she left the Ukraine
and travelled to Germany
before the outbreak of World War II –
hanging, today, in an ornate frame
appropriate to the Old World.

Growing up I never asked
detailed questions about it.
Why should I? What
more could she say
except it was herself,
her mother and older brother.

Now that my mother is dead
I look closely at what
I actually inherited –
at what appears to be a montage
of three people photographed
separately, coloured and overlapped,

their embroidered shirts
and blouses cross-stitched in rural style.
My mother, the only one smiling,
looking like a teenager,
wears a red ribbon or choker,
has white flowers in her hair.

Her brother, Peter, pale-skinned,
in the middle, looks shy.
'He was the kindest man
I knew,' she once told me.

'I named you after him.'
My grandmother Anna – her hair
tied back in a scarf –
stares placidly, head tilted
slightly to the right.

In my quietest moments
the portrait hangs in my mind
and does not fade away – as other possessions
I've acquired over the years
fall into insignificance
like dirt on the floor
waiting to be swept away.

Three faces that belong to me
as well as to themselves
and whom I'll live with for the rest of my life,
assembled as a portrait
that once belonged to my mother –
that she carried with her
like an exit visa from one life
and passport to another.